Working Guys
A Transmasculine Sex Worker Anthology

Edited by: Jack V Parker

Authors: Jack V Parker, Eddy, Rob Starkers, Liam, Arc D, Omar, Felix Mufti, Julian Yang, Faye, Mischa, Mx Dagger, A, Mister Saul/Jackson King, Ron Beastly, Dakota Nevaeh, Rush, Eric, Sunan, Trip Richards, and contributors who have chosen to remain anonymous.

Content Warnings

Sensitive topics will be discussed throughout this book, which some readers may find distressing. The submissions and additional chapters should be expected to contain discussion of sexuality and sexual acts, with some mentions being graphic in nature. All of the submissions will involve discussion of the sale of sexual services. The submissions will also sometimes include slurs, in the context of quoting bigoted comments or reclamation.

For each essay, more specific warnings will be provided at the back of this book. None of the essays or personal narratives included have been censored, thus some authors have chosen to share their personal traumas. Reading these accounts may be upsetting to readers with similar experiences, or those who are sensitive to the topics.

The sexual anatomy of transmasculine people will also be mentioned throughout the text, and a mixture of terms will be used by different authors.

This list covers some of the potentially triggering topics covered in this book and is not exhaustive: transphobia, homophobia, racism, ableism, fatphobia, misogyny, gender dysphoria, misgendering, hate crimes, sexual assault, physical assault, poverty, intrusive thoughts, dissociation.

Table of Contents

Introduction

Whatever kind of sex work we engage in, from stripping to escorting to making porn, there are parts of our work that only other sex workers instinctively understand. Cultural taboos around sexuality which treat it as sacred, within the context of capitalism, unite us all as people who charge for sexual services. To survive the stigma surrounding our work, sex workers build communities. These communities often have an overwhelming gender skew towards women, cis and trans, because women are much more likely to do sex work than men. For this reason, our communities often lack support or resources that are specific to the issues transmasculine sex workers face.

The lack of these resources for transmasculine sex workers is never the fault of women or transfeminine non-binary people. Comparisons that imply transfeminine people have an easier time in sex work because of their relative visibility are foolish, because all trans sex workers face transphobia combined with whorephobia and the hypervisibility that transfeminine sex workers face puts them at further risk. The hatred that is encouraged towards transfeminine sex workers makes them into targets.

Transmasculine sex workers still have unique challenges to deal with, alongside sharing some with our transfeminine sisters and siblings, many of which are the result of being invisibilized. Advertising becomes much more difficult when potential clients don't even have a mental concept of what a trans man is, or when they presume any androgynous non-binary person must be transfeminine. Testosterone can cause vaginal atrophy which makes it harder for many of us to see a large volume of clients. These struggles can be discussed without the implication that cis women or transfeminine people are responsible for them, because they *aren't*.

Gender, in both identity and presentation, has a profound impact on everyone's experience of sex work. It changes whether brothels will accept us to work in them, the level of demand for our pornographic content, and how much people are willing to pay us. As a niche population within an already marginalized minority, it can be hard to pick through the literature which exists about sex workers to find trans men and transmasculine non-binary people sharing their stories. Transmasculine people who are just beginning their careers in sex work, or who dabble in it out of necessity, may assume that it won't be a viable way to make money because they see so few models for what a successful transmasculine sex worker looks like.

Early on in my transition, I discovered a zine named *Trans Rentboys: Love Don't Pay the Rent*[1] and became fascinated by it. It was only 13 pages and included a small handful of transmasculine sex workers,

---

1 *Trans Rentboys: Love Don't Pay the Rent*, 2014, created by Sex Worker Open University.

but I was enamoured. I had never seen someone acknowledge the difference in the atmosphere and style between male and female sex work, or read such matter-of-fact recollections of the ever-repeating conversations we have with clients to explain what kind of trans we are. After I devoured that zine, I wanted more and couldn't find it. Articles that included our perspectives were sanitized and focused on aspects of our work that would shock people, many being authored by non sex workers, whereas I wanted to hear about the monotony and everyday experiences of other workers. I dragged myself to sex worker events and remained on the look-out for other trans people to chat to, emboldened by the knowledge that I was not alone.

Once I began to talk about what it has been like for me to sell sex, especially in public settings after beginning to transition, I realized how many things were different for me because I'm transmasculine. I ceased to struggle with changes in the UI and price hikes from some of the most popular escorting sites, because they were almost useless to me for getting clients once I was listed as male. Hotel staff not longer suspected me of being a hooker any time I showed up to meet a client, since I was either passing as a guy or assumed to be a butch lesbian. Violent interactions with clients became more common, but so did bookings where I spent time chatting with older queer men about gay history and felt content while I got them off. Hiding my face had become pointless because there are so few openly trans men advertising as escorts that I would be easy to find and recognize anyway.

My transness has impacted the way I work so much that I previously opted to speak exclusively about selling sex and making porn prior to my transition.

Anything that included working as a man or being non-binary was a deviation from the narratives that are still barely accepted by liberal feminists, such as the idea that sex work is a form of female empowerment or that sex workers are a cohesive sisterhood of marginalized women demanding freedom from criminalization. I didn't want to risk being dismissed by people I could convince to support sex workers rights. Persuading others of the need for the full decriminalization of sex work, as well as shutting down whorephobia, seemed like more important concerns than the unique challenges I face in sex work due to my gender.

Eventually, I began to allow the context of my transness to invade my tirades about the stigma against sex workers. This was more of a compulsion than a conscious choice. I was infuriated by every little instance of misgendering from within my own community, sick of stifling myself, and I needed an outlet to discuss the intersection of transphobia with the discrimination I was facing for being a sex worker.

For me, being a non-binary trans guy is inextricable from my identity as a sex worker. I cannot talk about how I began selling sex without outing myself as trans, because the way I was treated was strongly linked to the fact I was viewed as a girl, and I cannot pass for a cis woman when public speaking. My advertising methods since transitioning have shifted to mimic those of cis men who sell sex, separating me further from cis women in the industry, and so I cannot even anonymously discuss my current experience of sex work without outing myself in that way too. The stories I told when I began public speaking, about doing sex work pre-transition, were always impacted by the context my audience had of my current gender.

Anyone who would only lessen their vitriol against sex workers when we play along with the shallow, cissexist and bioessentialist beliefs they hold will always fall short of being a useful ally. Fellow queer sex workers encouraged me, assuring me that if anything there weren't *enough* trans guys opening up about doing sex work. Allies of trans people, who were uninformed about sex work, started to listen to what I had to say and advocate for sex workers and spread the word in a domino effect.

Emboldened, I started to speak about how I have been devalued as a hooker since I came out. Other transmasculine sex workers have nodded along as I divulged the impact of having a much smaller client pool of mostly queer men on my income. I see the value in speaking up about my life as a transmasculine person and a sex worker now, since I know how much I'd have appreciated learning about other people like me when I was new to it. I would have been more prepared for expectations that I stop charging extra for anal, or for the fact that people can find my escorting ads so easily because there are barely a dozen people advertising as trans men in my area.

What I still struggle with is the idea that I am taking up space where my sister sex workers, cis and trans, could be sharing their stories. There are more of them, they are the primary targets of anti sex work laws which are built upon a foundation of misogyny, and thus I shy away from sharing my perspective when they are willing to share theirs instead. Panels of speakers or line-ups at events often seek to fill certain demographic slots, including a space for at least one trans person, and I wonder if the trans community would be better served by a trans woman taking that opportunity instead of me.

What we really need is more representation of trans sex workers in general, with an understanding that no individual trans person can be a spokesperson for our entire community. My inclusion should never mean a transfeminine person loses out, and all kinds of trans sex workers have unique things to share.

Despite my neuroses about the most effective kinds of sex worker activism and my anxiety about stepping on the toes of others, I do recognize that there is a need for more information about transmasculine people in sex work for those who seek it. I know that trans men and various non-binary people with masculine identities are selling sex; I come across them constantly. As someone who brings up being a hooker to anyone who asks me what I do for a living, and who socializes with a lot of other trans people, I'm a magnet for transmasculine sex workers. They contact me online, open up to me in waiting rooms to get HRT injections, and I meet them at social events. I shouldn't be their only lifeline or source of information, as a singular person with a limited experience.

The pieces of writing in this book, including essays and personal narratives, are intended to fill in some of the gaps in our collective knowledge about transmasculine sex work. The writers come from a range of backgrounds with diverse sexualities and ages, in the hopes of creating a snapshot transmasculine experiences selling sex and porn and other sexual services. I am not alone in wanting to speak up, and this anthology allows us all to take advantage of the shared opportunity.

You will find that many of the contributors to this anthology have chosen to remain anonymous or written under pseudonyms. For some, identifying pieces of information have been omitted or changed. This is because speaking openly about being a sex worker carries a harsh stigma and can have legal and social consequences. Transmasculine sex workers are a group at an even higher risk of being outed and having our real identities connected to our work names, due to the fact that we are a smaller population that can be filtered through more easily to find us. Allowing contributors to remain anonymous means that those who cannot be open about their profession in their private lives are still able to provide us with their stories.

Transmasculine people may be a minority among those who do sex work, but a significant proportion of transmasculine people sell sex and we deserve to be understood and access support and community. I hope that this anthology will provide people with a resource to understand us better, and that it will serve as a balm to transmasculine sex workers like myself who ache with the desire to find others who understand us.

Submission 1, by Eddy

Embracing Ambiguity and Complexity in Sex Work

Eddy (@edftmxxx) is a queer trans sex worker living in London. He started meeting clients and making porn in 2019/2020, with his work centring pleasure, pride, and inclusivity. Outside of work, he loves reading queer fiction, lifting weights, cooking vegan feasts, watching horror films, and hosting board games afternoons.

Whenever anyone asks what I do for work, I say very directly that I'm a sex worker. I'm in the privileged position of not needing to say vaguely that I work in customer service, or in online marketing, or to invent a cover story (apparently accounting is the best one, since people are unlikely to ask follow-up questions). Growing up, I never pictured myself with a serious career. Whether this was an individual personality trait or a valid response to the portrayal of trans people in the media—as objects of pity or laughter, with sex work as the most common job, or destined to die young, probably by murder—I can't say.

What comes next depends heavily on who I'm talking to.

To my parents, I'm quick to emphasise the perks of the job, such as the fact that I'm able to pay into my pension each month, and also to gloss over the potential negatives. I might try to portray my job as something idyllic, to reassure them that I'm never putting myself in any danger. Really, I don't give them many details at all.

To other sex workers I might focus on the horrible stories in some situations, when I'm in need of support from people I know will understand and sympathise without questioning the validity of the job itself.

To my friends, I'm more measured; they might hear the occasional funny story, or an achievement I'm proud of—but again, I don't generally reveal many details.

To strangers, I try to be as direct as possible, with the rest of the conversation being directed by their initial reaction.

The truth is that I often feel deeply ambivalent about my work; I'm torn between the desire to defend it (because I enjoy it) and the desire to critique it (because it's work, and I would prefer not to need to work, or at least to be able to do so in better conditions). In all of these conversations, I never lie about my work, but I find it difficult to convey my thoughts effectively, while avoiding narratives that speak in absolutes: sex work being wholly degrading and exploitative, or sex work being entirely unproblematic and enjoyable. For me it's somewhere in the middle—often a little of both. Despite my candour, I fully understand the desire—and frequently, the need—to conceal the truth.

Stigma towards sex workers is still rampant, often crossing into active persecution. I discovered this for myself in 2022, when I attempted to visit the US. I arrived at the airport in Atlanta, and was stopped at border control. After scanning my face and passport, alarms went off, and I was taken by security to a detention room to wait. Eventually I was told that I would not be allowed to enter the country. My visa was cancelled. I was held in a cell overnight and sent back to the UK the following evening. The reason was that I had worked as a sex worker in the UK, despite the fact that I had broken no laws here and was not suspected of intending to work in the US (I have family in the US and had provided their details). It's not totally clear how I was flagged, but appears to be either face recognition or the sale of data from websites I had used to advertise. I realised only afterwards the extent to which this happens to sex workers trying to travel to the US.

How to square this with the mundanity of my daily life? I was treated as a criminal, made to answer invasive questions, and banned from the entire country (for at least ten years, by the way!). Suddenly my openness and pride in my work felt a little less inconsequential. Here I was being told in no uncertain terms that my work should not be a source of pride; I was being told, 'We don't want people like you in our country.' My experience was awful and traumatic—and I'm white and a native English speaker. I can only imagine how much worse it is for other people.

I was thinking: how can the response to my work be so extreme, when the reality is so mundane? Aside from the sex element, my work routine isn't unusual. I have my own business, I pay my taxes, and I spend most of my working days sitting in front of my laptop.

However, I'm conscious that when I explain my job in these terms, there's the danger of giving the impression that I'm distancing myself from sex workers whose lives are drastically different from mine. Although in some ways I'm very privileged, our struggles are collective.

I catch myself trying to justify my job to others, not out of any sense of shame (on the contrary, I'm proud of what I've achieved), but out of a desire to legitimise it. I find myself emphasising the ordinary nature of my work, which may be true, but it's worth interrogating whether this is the sole aim. It's almost as if I need to couch my work and daily activities in concepts that fit the expectation of a 'respectable' job.

How is this any different from attempts to assimilate into cishet society—attempts I used to make, before I grew more comfortable with my transness and began to be proud of my differences, rather than seeking validation from other people.

In order to be a man, I don't need to reject or scorn femininity. I'm me, and I'm a man, and under that broad and fluid definition, I'm at times masculine and at times feminine, but at all times proudly trans and proudly queer. The tendency among some binary trans people to conform to the expectations of cishet culture is one I sympathise with, because being trans is difficult, and when there is the chance to exist quietly and stealthily, life can be much simpler (especially where, as is often the case, there is a safety need). However, it is possible to assimilate if that's right or necessary for an individual, while continuing to advocate for anyone whose gender expression is loudly and overtly transgressive; to avoid drawing boundaries: I'm trans, or gay, or queer—but not like that. The issue here is not other trans and nonbinary people, whose struggles may be distinct but overlapping, and whose abilities to be stealth may be much lower or non-existent. Rather the issue is a society that demands conformity and rigidity, and attempts at every turn to control and restrict our bodies.

Similarly, even when being honest about the daily realities of being a sex worker—for example, that 90% of the job is admin—I shouldn't need to do so just to aspire to someone else's definition of what constitutes a respectable career. This is just another way of entrenching class differences and attempting to distance myself from other sex workers; again: I do it, but not like that. To be clear, this is wrong. I stand in solidarity with all workers, all migrants and illegal workers, those working at all levels and for any amount of money, those camming to pay for higher education and those streetwalking to feed and house themselves. All sex work is valid, at least insofar as it's all work and therefore all deserving of workers' rights and improved working conditions. Sex work is sex, but more importantly, it's work. It's no-one else's place—including the government—to put restrictions on what I do with my body.

For me, these doubly marginalised existences are intertwined and inseparable and feed into a larger drive to be as loud as I can about who I am: queer, trans, gay, and a sex worker, and I wouldn't change any of it.

The answers I give in each of these conversations are all true. It feels impossible sometimes to convey the nuances of the work in one conversation, but I'm conscious too that workers in very few other industries are asked so continually to defend and justify their work. Again: it's work. Sometimes it's good, sometimes it's bad—in the same way as your job, probably—but none of these factors takes away from the fact that I need to do it to pay my bills. I'm not desperate and depressed, nor am I constantly feeling empowered and validated.

The sexual validation and body confidence the job gives me can coexist with the frustration I feel with disrespectful clients, and with the joy I get when a trans person tells me my content has helped them, and with the anger I have about the injustice of the treatment of sex workers convicted for 'brothel-keeping' after working in pairs for safety.

Despite often fraught debates about the work, there aren't easy answers, although at the forefront of any discussions should always be harm reduction and the prioritisation of the welfare and well-being of sex workers ourselves—not policymakers, or feminists commenting on the symbolism of buying sex. Sex workers' voices should be platformed above all others— with space allowed for the kind of ambivalence I've explored here. We don't need to unequivocally love our jobs to demand safer and more supportive working environments.

Chapter 1: Female Personas

Not unlike drag performers, sex workers often engage in exaggerated gender performances when providing sexual services. As women are the most sought after by the predominantly straight male client pool, trans men and transmasculine non-binary people frequently pose as a gender that is not our own to attract them. We construct female personas. The clothing we wear for work becomes a costume, the make-up a kind of disguise, and we turn into skilled drag queens in guerilla performances. Some of the contributors to this anthology have also had this experience, myself among them.

I have heard from a flood of transmasculine people who are (or have been) "cis for pay". Dozens of transmasculine sex workers and former sex workers reached out to me, as a direct result of an article I wrote about trans men being a hidden population within sex work[2], and I interviewed many of them. They seldom continued to do sex work to the same extent after coming out, most having quit entirely before they began

---

2   *The hidden trans men in sex work*, 23rd May 2023, Irresistible Damage, a magazine for gay and bi trans men/mascs.

any form of medical transition, and none had spoken about the experience publicly for fear of being ridiculed or viewed as less masculine. The few who did continue to do frequent sex work often had dazzling insights on gender performativity, in light of the contract they experienced before and after coming out.

Through meeting so many other sex workers like myself, I was reminded of my own early experiences selling sex whilst claiming to be a cis girl and woman. I lacked the awareness I have now, so I believed that my presumed lesbianism was the reason I felt the need to play a character for my clients. Hearing that other people also used mental gymnastics to explain away their dysphoria when writing their escorting ads or taking nudes for their subscription sites brought me comfort.

Meeting (mostly cis) sex workers who did not construct a separate work persona confounded me, at the beginning of my sex work career. I had universalized my own experience as if it applied to all cis women who sold sex or made porn, not yet realizing that I was trans. Having a masculine gender identity had a huge impact on how I felt about acting as a woman to seduce straight men, but I presumed that the disconnect I felt between my true self and the roleplay I did for work was inherent to being a sex worker. Once corrected, I felt like I was doing something wrong. I felt alone.

After I came out, I began to find other transmasculine people in similar circumstances. They confided in me that they also constructed female personas. I wasn't regarded with confusion when I talked about playing a role when I sold sex or filmed a masturbation video for my subscribers, complete with girlish giggles and moans that sounded wrong coming out of my mouth.

One young trans man I spoke with told me that he views selling sex as being more like an "acting gig" than anything else. He said, "I often talk about myself by my work name, in the third person. I'll talk about what she is like. She isn't really me, she's this flirty girl I made up to take money from oblivious men." He broke from association with his work persona to such an extent that he said he felt no discomfort referring to her in feminine terms.

Since so many sex workers use a stage name for work, as a way to protect our identities while dodging stigma and state surveillance, it becomes easier to think of our work self as a different person. In the case where this persona is a different gender to us, we are primed to develop an alter ego or to treat our work persona as a part we're playing instead of reducing it to a pseudonym. I think about my peer saying "she isn't really me" in reference to the performance he embodies when he sells sex and it resonates with me.

The reality that many transmasculine people put on a complex feminine act, rather than simply claiming to be women and still acting like ourselves, raises the question of why we do so. Feminine women tend to be considered more desirable by clients and customers, but changing all of our mannerisms and lying about our hobbies isn't necessary to attract those men. Why build a character when we could settle for a feminine overlay, complete with only a name and a dress and maybe a wig?

The dysphoria elicited by being viewed as a woman in such an intimate setting contributes to the sensation that the client is only interacting with an imitation of a person. I interviewed a trans man who has been selling sex for longer than I've been alive, and he recalled making up new stories every time his clients asked him why he started escorting. "They'd say, 'why is a gorgeous girl like you doing something like this?' and I'd come up with a new lie each time. I earned myself tips if the story was sad enough!" When I questioned what prompted him to answer at all, or to make up new things in place of sticking to the same falsehood every time, he responded, "They were asking about the gorgeous girl they were seeing, not about me. I had fun with it!"

I only came to understand that sex workers could feel like our clients were interacting with us, and not just the simulacrum other transmasculine sex workers have described to me, once I came out as trans to my clients. Suddenly I wasn't doing drag for work any more; it was more akin to regular customer service. I am still polite to clients in a way that I am not in my daily life, and I don't share most forms of personal information, but my mannerisms are real and my clothing doesn't feel like a costume. It is difficult to say whether I could have been doing that all along, relying on my clients seeing what they wanted to see and their obliviousness to my internal identity if I didn't mention it. On the other hand, the dysphoria of being misgendered would be so much more extreme if it occurred whilst I was being myself.

It is possible that these female personas are an overcompensation resulting from a belief that many trans people have, that others can sense something is off about us. A cis female sex worker might feel comfortable presenting as a tomboy whilst a transmasculine sex worker becomes convinced that their transness will be discovered if they allow themselves a sliver of gender non-conformity. Meanwhile, clients are frequently oblivious and are likely to project whatever they desire onto the sex workers they see, in the absence of something extreme to jar them out of their fantasy.

Personal style and preference also contribute to whether a sex worker may feel the need to adjust their presentation to appeal to clients. For transmasculine people who like to wear feminine attire and are not medically transitioning, creating a separate character for work may be superfluous. One non-binary sex worker I surveyed spoke about their gender presentation and said that, "Everyone thinks I'm a woman anyway and I can't be bothered to dress and act differently to make them see that I'm non-binary. I shouldn't owe anyone masculinity." When it came to the question of whether or not they change that presentation for clients, they answered, "I mostly do whatever I want and they react the same as everyone else, thinking I'm a woman. My wardrobe is all 'women's clothes' and I have tits and that's enough."

How feminine a sex worker is expected to be will heavily depend on other aspects of the character they are playing, on the kind of sexual services they offer, and on their class and race and age and body type and whether they are disabled. Clients are likely to have racist and ableist and classist expectations and beliefs about femininity, these other forms of bigotry interacting with their misogyny and creating specific standards.

Cis and trans workers alike have to contend with how clients anticipate they will behave and what they expect of someone they view as a woman. These differing expectations include, but are not limited to: having higher standards for how feminine women of colour should be, viewing certain expensive attire as essential to an elevated level of femininity, seeing youth and femininity as being bound together.

Whether a client has high standards for the femininity of some sex workers they see does not directly correlate with how feminine transmasculine sex workers of those demographics will act. Maintaining a feminine exterior can be time-consuming, expensive, and exhausting. In some cases, that standard that many clients have becomes so high that it stops being worth it for the sex worker to try at all, and the female persona collapses into a simple claim to be a woman regardless of presentation. How successful this is likely to be, in terms of attracting and keeping paying clients, will continue to be impacted by the client's bigoted views on how women of different demographics should behave.

Workplaces for sex workers will also encourage the development of very feminine personas, for sex workers who are not entirely independent. Strip clubs frequently refuse to hire more than one or two performers of colour, have limits on dress sizes, reject those with visible disabilities, and require all strippers to be below a certain age. These restrictions are sometimes malleable, but they become less so if the sex worker is openly gender non-conforming. I asked one black non-binary worker to share why they feel so much pressure to be hyper-feminine for work, and they responded, "That's because I'm the only black girl – not that I'm really a girl – at every club I work at. Loads of people want my place and I need to be perfect to keep it. I spend so much on nails and lashes that it makes a big dent in what I take home."

Equally, sex workers who do low interaction forms of sex work or build specific niches for themselves may be able to ease up on how feminine their female persona is. Some transmasculine sex workers who do this can forgo it almost entirely and merely claim to be a woman, without changing any of their behaviour. Short of coming out and doing sex work whilst openly trans, this is likely to be the scenario which causes the least dysphoria, though it has the trade-off of the hard work required to train and advertise for a niche form of sex work, or spending the time to bring in customers for the low interaction kind. This can include making porn which caters to consumers interested in tomboys, offering phone sex for hard kinks, selling sploshing services, becoming a foot fetish model, and more.

"Bringing my audience from camming over to phone sex was the best thing I ever did. I use a pre-transition picture to go with my profile and no-one sees me," is what a former cam model told me about his move towards a form of sex work with a lower client pool, which he did so that he could cut his hair and stop wearing lingerie instead of a binder. However, he admits that it has made his work harder in other ways. "I hardly get any new clients and the ones from camming are dropping off. I'm in a transition phase, pun intended, while I find new work before the phone sex clients run out."

Ultimately, the belief that there are a relatively small number of trans men and transmasculine non-binary people doing sex work can be attributed to the way so many of us hide behind acting as if we are women. Speaking to even a small number of transmasculine sex workers reveals this flaw. You cannot find the number of transmasculine people using an escorting website or working at a strip club or making porn when so many of us are actively lying about our gender to keep our earnings up. Researchers will get false information from us too, because we are unlikely to trust them not to report it in a way that will out us, and they should recognize this.

In the period of time when I was still working under a female persona, I only came out to my closest friends and a limited number of other (predominantly also trans) sex workers. It is much easier for us to find each other, by word of mouth and spotting each other at events within the sex worker community, than for anyone else to find and study us. Any estimates of the total transmasculine population in sex work are hardly worth the time they take to read.

Presentation and gender identity are not one in the same thing, and this is doubly true when someone's presentation is being altered by an additional outside force. Sex workers' female personas are not built to be easy to see through; if we are armed with the knowledge that transmasculine people use them, we can be prepared to recognize them for who they actually are underneath, when they reveal themselves.

Submission 2, by Rob Starkers

Dressed Resembling A Girl

Rob Starkers is a drag king, underworld dandy, semi-retired sex worker and writer. He has gone by many names, worn many costumes and fooled a lot of people into thinking he's someone else. In his spare time, he can usually be found at a drag show, in a graveyard or rewatching Ripley (2024) on Netflix.

He has previously appeared in Truth and Lies: An Anthology of Writing & Art by Sex Workers (2022) under another name.

If gender is a performance, then it's amazing I haven't been booed off the stage yet. When Shakespeare wrote that "one man in his time plays many parts" I don't think he quite envisioned the parts I would play. Though, in fairness, in his day men played women all the time.

I took my first working name from him – Miranda. I needed something slightly upmarket but not too niche. Since selling a fantasy to men was a "brave new world" and I was a pretentious idiot, it just seemed to fit.

"You're everything a woman should be. A beautiful, submissive English rose."

A prospective client comments this on one of my photos. I show this to my partner at the time. They squeal and then chuckle in a low voice for a good thirty seconds.

"It's amazing how little they know you?" they laugh, when they finally catch their breath.

"Can't they see you're a twink?" There's genuine surprise in their voice.

Since you're curious, I'm tall, with elfin features. Pale, high cheekbones, cupid's bow mouth. When I was a kid and playing Lord of the Rings, I always wanted to be Legolas. I never wanted to cut my long hair; I always wanted to be pretty. A pretty girl, pretty boy, pretty...question mark? I don't really care what strangers read me as, as long it's it's "pretty".

I'm not a girl but not quite a man either (a lesser-known Britney Spears hit). I exist in a liminal space, the late night supermarket of gender, shelved somewhere between the houseplants and kombucha. My gender is fluid – specifically, a pornstar martini in flavour and aesthetic.

I don't hate "her" - "her" being my work persona. She's a fantasy. I could never be her, although I do a good impression! She's high femme, bubbly, she exists only in strip clubs, dungeons and hotel rooms. Miranda is a drag act. A class act. I was raised within sight and sound of Bow's bells. Miranda is Eliza Doolittle curated for the Henry Higginses of the world. My type is like me – trans, ethereal, a little out of time. My clients are anything but; older, greyer and ordinary. Frequently named Ian.

"I'd love to see you outside of work? What's your real number? Your real name?"

Every working girl has heard this a thousand times before. But with me it hits a little different. I know their fantasy because I sold it to them, wholesale. They expect me to be perching on a bar stool somewhere, waiting for them to buy me a drink. Meanwhile, I haunt gay bars and DIY punk venues, often actual graveyards just for the peace and quiet. I'm not "unrecognisable", but they would likely never come across the real me even if they tried.

I remember the first time I properly got into boy drag. I accentuated my eyebrows and cheekbones, hinted at the possibility of facial hair but could neither confirm nor deny. One of the proudest moments of my life was seeing the look on my flatmate's face when I flounced into the living room that day. A double-take, a miniscule eyebrow raise. I'd seen that reaction from straight men from the second I hit puberty, but from a gay man? A first. Affirming.

Dressed Resembling A Girl. Whether that's where it originates or not, from Shakespeare's day to the present, it's my reality. It's how I navigate the world, for my comfort, my safety and... frequently my own amusement.

Submission 3, by Liam

"Only Women Sell Sex"

Liam is a trans guy who has been selling sex since before he began to medically transition. He is currently dedicated to staying sober and in therapy, putting himself first, and refusing to let judgemental people determine his self worth.

     A friend of mine told me that he struggled to gender me correctly when I first came out. All my other friends, including a couple of trans friends, talked around the reasons they would slip up with pronouns – I knew the real reasons were my high-pitched voice and a feminine physique. He didn't avoid saying why. His reasons were different. He told me that he struggled to see me as a man because I sell sex. The words gave me flashes of what I was sure he imagined, a picture of me in lingerie and laying on my back under a client, and I found it hard to see the version of myself that I hid behind for work as anything other than a woman too. What he said to me had spread the sickness and I felt unsure in my identity.

     I pretended to be a woman for work, so people saw me as one outside of it too.

     Things only got worse after my friend told me how he saw me. Feeling defeated made me want to give in and use my femininity to my advantage to make money. I felt like everyone saw me as a woman anyway and it couldn't hurt any worse. I didn't see any other way to pay my bills. This is my first time telling someone this story and the temptation is so strong to start listing out reasons I tortured myself like this, so no-one reading it invalidates me like my friend did.

Glam looks turned into my signature. I turned into a drag queen for work (and a caricature of the girl I used to be). I got tired of putting on lashes every morning and decided to get lash extensions. It didn't matter that I felt dysphoric about them – I though no-one would take me seriously as a man with my normal lashes in the first place. My friend would view me as a woman for looking through my lashes at my client while I sucked him off with or without extensions. I had my nails painted with the same reasoning. The clients loved my look, told me it was super porno and more than one of them affectionately called me a bimbo.

The friends who misgendered me some of the time started misgendering me all the time and I stopped correcting them. Some of them drifted away from me and a few of my friends seemed to forget that I'd ever come out to them. It was like I'd announced I was detransitioning and that I'd been wrong about being trans all along, except I hadn't. I felt crazy and I had no idea how to speak up. I got more timid and femme-presenting and that was enough for them to give up on seeing me as a man, so I pretty much gave up on it myself and sank into a depression.

Any kind of social or medical transition started to feel impossible and I let my dreams of living as a man fade away from me. I was trapped inside of this male fantasy of a woman and I hated her with everything I had. Drugs helped me to avoid thinking about it and I stopped doing my make-up so I didn't have to look at myself in the mirror. I would put on lipstick without looking and with bright lips and lash extensions clients reacted the same as when I spent two hours on beating my face. I don't know if they ever cared or if I was making myself look like a clown all the time for no reason.

I mixed drugs and alcohol enough that I started to get sick all the time. Lots of my bookings turned into party bookings. I did lines of coke with one client and got drunk with another straight after (and got billed for throwing up on the hotel carpet). I didn't feel like any gender when I was high or drunk. The drugs let me be no-one.

I took days off when I was too tired to see any more clients and I'd earned enough to pay for everything. Flicking through social media endlessly was comforting and helped me drift through my hangovers and the come down from coke. I skipped past any mentions of trans people on my feed.

On one night off of work, depressed, I scrolled onto the Facebook page of the friend who told me that he couldn't see me as a man because I sell sex. I clicked on his profile and his most recent post was a photo of him standing next to our mutual friend – a trans man who came out after I did and started to pass as a man some time between when we lost touch and the moment the picture was taken. I was so frustrated I started crying. I was so angry that having this job meant that couldn't be me in the picture.

Seeing the post pushed me to do something. I cut my hair that night into a really ugly bob and then shaved it all off the next morning. I got a bunch of oil and make-up remover in my eyes trying to get my lash extensions off. Over the next week I lost most of my regular clients (they thought I was having a Britney-esque breakdown) and started to get way less phone calls and texts showing an interest. It was quick and definitive and never got back to the level it was at before I changed my profile.

The aftermath was that I had to move into a shared apartment with a load of people to find a cheaper place to rent. I got onto testosterone through informed consent and paid for my prescriptions as the first priority, eating ramen noodles or not eating at all so I could afford it. I kept seeing clients and told some I was a tomboy and some that I was trans and I earned way less. Took months of trying, but I even got a part time vanilla job.

Some of my old friends have tried to get in touch again since all this (the friend who started my miserable detransition spiral included). I kind of pass and the old friends I've met with all use he/him without a problem. I've learned from my mistakes with being too open and now I lie to everyone that my part time job is the only job I have and that I quit sex work to transition. They don't feminize me in their minds by mentally putting me in the role of a woman selling sex in the last trashy article they read or film they watched. It sucks that I don't get to enjoy it properly because I know things would be different if I was totally honest.

I'm angry that my friends couldn't support me when I needed it most. I could have worked as a woman and not spent half my money on drugs to cope if my friends took me seriously about being a man. I should have had a place to go to vent and get validation. Then I'd have money now for a nicer apartment and some savings towards top surgery, instead of damage to the inside of my nose. My transition would have been smoother and losing clients wouldn't have made it so I couldn't afford to eat every day.

My friend, who saw me as a woman because he knew I sold sex, made me feel like I'd be a woman until I found some other way to pay my bills. He made me think there was no point in transition if I couldn't drag myself out of selling sex – something I never liked doing in the first place and only ever did because I couldn't find any other job.

I started to believe that selling sex made me a woman.

Last week one of my clients found me through Grindr and called me a faggot during sex.

Submission 4, by Arc D

Arc D (they/them) is a mischief boi, a transmasc sex worker, and a multimedia artist who's been involved in sex work in various settings over the past 4 years.

Sex work, earning a living, and exploring my transness are deeply intertwined for me. It's difficult to talk about one without referencing others. When I first started working, I had already come out as non-binary; however, I was still working under the guise of a cis woman. Coming from a Middle Eastern country, I had never considered any other possibilities until I migrated to Germany.

As a woman, you have more options within sex work, even though being pursued as a woman is suffocating. There are some advantages to performing as one; it offers some protection, as it may make clients less likely to exercise power over you compared to when they perceive you as trans— so, adapting to heteronormative structures and performing as a woman gave me a sense of control and safety during work, in comparison to being open about my identity. When you meet multiple clients every day, you have to assume they are homophobic unless proven otherwise. In the context of where I came from, sex work is only considered 'legal' if you register in a brothel. So, it's not surprising that most of the work occurs in illegal and highly life-threatening conditions. Trans workers are the most severely and disproportionately affected as a result. They are subjected to constant threats, harassment, and raids on their homes by police and other authorities.

Living in a Western setting has made it easier to deal with the vulnerability of starting my transition. I can operate under better conditions here – by claiming my rights and being free from the government's constant threats. It certainly makes a difference. Despite my growing desire to see changes in my body and voice, in the past I just kept working and never allowed myself to think more. Now, having access to hormones and being able to control my transition, things make a lot more sense and this brings clarity; even though I'm highly confident while working, things that made me shy, hide, and confused in my personal life are becoming a lot clearer.

Still, I have so much compassion for the past that led me here, because I genuinely think this would not have been possible without the decision to move and gain access to better conditions rather than just those needed to survive. The system for workers here is far from functioning well, as there are many gaps when working as a migrant and navigating the registered legal conditions. However, now that my process has started and I believe in myself enough to feel whole on a daily basis, things have become manageable. Finally, being openly trans, I really can't care less what people think about me. That is certainly new and refreshing because it means that being many things at the same time does not necessarily have to be a bad thing. Building a life from that is a huge privilege one can use for something meaningful. That's how I feel about my work; it gives me a sense of purpose – small or big, it doesn't matter – being there for those going through their own struggles and making myself a life out of this 'mess' is already good enough.

Submission 5, by Anonymous

Plausible Deniability

Anonymous is a mostly straight man wrapped up like a genderfuck fantasy for gay and bi men with internalized homophobia, a lightning rod for sexual discovery, and is probably taller than you.

What I sell, more than sex itself, is plausible deniability. I am the "no homo" version of fucking a man, for most of my clients. I'm the "it's not gay because there are no balls to touch" exception that gets them out of questioning their sexualities. I cultivate these clients on purpose. It's funny, if a little sad, and in my experience repressed bisexual and gay men give better head.

They want to suck cock so they treat my t-dick like it is one, telling themselves it's okay because I have a pussy. A pussy they're paying no attention to, but its effect must have a radius. They're close enough. It's not gay as long as they remain transphobic enough to see me as a woman. At least in theory, they have to keep believing it, even if they never feel that way in the moment while they're fucking me.

Never mind that they chose me out of a sea of feminine cis women, it's not gay because I was born female! In public with our clothes on, everyone would see two men together and think of us as gay, but he'd never associate with me outside of this dingy flat and so he'll never have to reckon with that. He clings to his assertion that he's straight even as he puts me on my front and requests anal while he listens to me grunt, knowing that from the angle he's at there is no indication that I'm trans.

I've been a stepping stone before, to men without pussies who they fuck once they give up on denial. I've heard confessions next to me in bed, about youthful experimentation with boys that they still feel ashamed of and deny wanting any more. I've pegged clients and had them tell me they've always fantasized about a man fucking them but since they're straight they hadn't found a way to make it happen until finding me.

I laugh and I laugh and I laugh.

I sell these clients their plausible deniability without remorse. Their denial is not my problem. It is sad, if I think about it for too long, and it is funny. I collect the money of these closeted bisexual men and curse the homophobic world that makes them deny themselves as I smile at the way I profit from it. I think it would be more ethical to sell only sex. Selling plausible deniability pays more.

My advertisements are vague about my gender identity. I list myself as female and claim to be a genderless void. I talk about my pussy and my masculine energy and my deep voice and I never call myself trans. As long as they're paying me, I tell them that they can call me whatever they want. What I am outside of this world of providing sex doesn't matter. I earn money for my performance and I don't care if they call me a woman to make themselves feel better about enjoying it.

Such is my confidence in myself and who I am as a man that clients do not ruin my enjoyment of the sex with their comments. I find their excuses for not being gay to be ridiculous and so their mutterings to convince themselves of the reasons they are heterosexual can't get to me.

The only gay sex I have is with men who pay me for it, most of whom would deny that the sex we have is gay at all. A type of "gay for pay" that one side is pretending doesn't count. For the right price I'm happy to allow them to cling onto those delusions until they're ready to let them go. I'll enable it. I'll participate in it.

Chapter 2: Popularity in Porn

Recent years have seen an increase in both the demand for porn featuring transmasculine people and the number of people creating it. This surge in popularity is partially due to a new wave of awareness of the existence of trans men among the porn-watching public; people can't search for types of bodies they are unaware of the existence of. Another factor is that individual sex workers have suddenly become capable of creating and distributing our own porn with ease, so we are no longer beholden to the discriminatory whims of large studios. Anyone who wants to record sexual content of themselves can do so, and they can charge for access or upload it to a tube site. When porn studios avoid us because they believe we aren't marketable, we prove them wrong.

On Pornhub, one of the most widely used tube porn sites, women are recorded as being much more likely than men to search for porn featuring trans men[3]. This doesn't mean they make up the majority of watchers, because women account for a smaller proportion of Pornhub users in general. Women also

---

3   *Transgender Porn Searches, Pornhub Insights.*

account for a massive proportion of viewers of gay male porn on Pornhub[4], and the transmasculine porn they view is often a subset of it. We don't even know what the prevalence of nonbinary people is among those searching for this kind of porn, nor how often the people searching for it are trans, because that information is not recorded. Cis men remain the demographic we cater to most strongly when crafting our porn.

The newfound visibility of transmasculine sex workers in porn has arrived faster than the technology and categories have caught up with us. Trans categories on porn sites are poorly labelled with transphobic words and often include videos with similar transphobic tags, defaulting to showing transfeminine performers because the category was originally created with them in mind and no consideration for other kinds of trans people. As the sites take time to adapt, both sex workers making content and viewers watching it have to work around a user interface that doesn't have us in mind.

Verification systems for uploading porn of ourselves also fail to account for gender transition occurring along the duration of our careers. When I tried to upload the bulk of my pre-transition videos to a few tube sites, intending to bring in ad revenue and use it as advertising at the same time, my uploads were flagged because the gender listed on my profile was not consistent with the gender of the performer present. Porn sites have trans categories and profit from the content we make, showing outward support, yet fail to think of us when designing basic rules for uploads. I would note that the person in the video was myself, thus giving me the right to post it, and I would get pop-up messages and e-

---

4   *Pride Insights 2024, Pornhub Insights.*

mails to warn me that my personal information did not match with the description and tags for the video. It took weeks to get through to someone on the moderation team for each site to resolve this, all of whom had their pronouns in their e-mail signatures.

Inquiring as to whether anyone else had similar issues with the UI of porn sites as a transmasculine person, I found a few who had their videos taken down because they began to look too masculine for moderators to believe they were the same person. Someone who had this issue multiple times told me, "I ended up having to change my gender marker on my ID sooner than I wanted to. I grew facial hair so fast on T and I kept getting flagged on porn sites and asked to upload ID and model release forms for the person in my videos, and it would take several tries because my photo ID had an F and I looked like a teenage girl on it. You'd think they'd add a note to my account internally or something after it happened so many times." A follow-up question about how he felt after repeatedly encountering the same problem got me an even more revealing answer. "I'd feel better if they fixed their transphobic site design instead of apologizing for the same mistake all the time."

Connecting to viewers is the next hurdle once we get our videos uploaded, which requires tagging and relying on the algorithm to get our videos out to the kinds of people who would be interested. To search for porn including transmasculine people, one of the few ways to reliably filter the results is to use the term "FTM", because this tag is usually only placed on videos featuring trans men and transmasculine performers. Although "trans man" or "transmasc" would be less medicalizing and more respectful, porn featuring trans women ends up being mixed into the results when these search terms are used.

Studios and individual sex workers alike will tag their videos with both "trans woman" and "trans man", knowing that many viewers won't use the right terms and will be transphobic enough not to view the trans people they watch as the gender they are. This reinforces their usage of the incorrect terms. Knowing what viewers type into their search bars, and what they're hoping to get from those searches, then has a knock-on effect to how sex workers tag their videos in the future. We've seen a huge increase in the prevalence of specific acronyms and terminology in usernames and profiles and tags, as a result. The market is saturated with transmasculine creators using "man with a pussy" and "bonus hole boi/boy" as our tag lines, with FTM and TS in our usernames.

Those catering to small audiences, who do not rely on the income from selling sexual content, can more easily make porn which appeals to them personally or that they want to see more of and avoid worrying so much about how they tag it. Viewership can take a back seat to quality – though many creators certainly manage to make pornographic masterpieces in spite of constraints related to staying popular. The smaller and more marginalized a group of sex workers are, the fewer of them have such privileges and the more difficult it can be to find well-produced porn featuring certain acts or people. Once a consumer manages to find porn with transmasculine people in it, through discovering sex workers advertising their subscription sites or on tube sites, they may be disappointed to see a distinct lack of variety in the acts and bodies shown.

44

Bottoming isn't so common in porn with transmasculine performers solely because it is their preference – it's what is expected and is what customers are most willing to pay for. As transmasculine people become an established demographic within porn, we're on shaky footing and so many of us play it safe and offer the same kind of content that we already see becoming popular. That isn't to say that trans men and transmasculine non-binary people never take on the role of the person doing the penetrating in the sexual content that can be found online, however it is much more difficult to find compared to clips of cis men topping us. Transmasculine people showing off their post-surgery dicks are even rarer. Our content is treated more as a subset of gay porn than its own separate genre, with the trans performers treated as if we're made to bottom because of our anatomy. In a strange reverse of the usual issue we see within media, there is a distinct lack of straight content.

When it comes to companies who are willing to include transmasculine people in their productions, they appear to choose the actors they work with according to some concerning criteria. There is a huge over-representation of white twinks being featured in trans porn that is so extreme that even very oblivious porn viewers notice it. A scroll through the likes of *FTMMen* or *Jockpussy* on the *FTMPlus* porn network will see you greeted with video after video of white trans men who are thin and smaller than the cis men they are partnered with. On some websites you'll find transmasculine porn actors of colour to be entirely absent. A lack of talented porn performers of all ethnicities is not the problem – racist standards within the porn industry are.

Something closer to the true variety of the trans community can be found when browsing through tags on social media to find sex workers to purchase content from, however this results in many performers being overlooked because customers have to go out of their way to search for them. If it doesn't occur to someone to look for fat black trans men offering JOI audio recordings or disabled Asian non-binary performers making roleplay videos, these gems among the sea of pornographic content go ignored. It shouldn't take so much effort, which customers are unlikely to expend when horny and looking to make a purchase that they can quickly get off to, to allow interested viewers to find videos showcasing performers of a plethora of races and ethnicities and body types.

Barring the few transmasculine sex workers who become minor celebrities through their porn, the vast majority of us have no hope of supporting ourselves financially with the money we make from selling subscriptions or videos alone. Not being able to cover all of our expenses exclusively by making porn, many transmasculine people end up mixing porn creation with in-person work. The less a particular transmasculine person is valued within porn and the more they are discriminated against in casting (and by bigoted potential customers), the more likely they are to find themselves pressured to branch out into other kinds of sex work.

Speaking about his difficulties making money through his porn as an Asian trans man, one fellow sex worker I interviewed said, "I had all these stars in my eyes in the beginning. I knew I was never gonna be the Asian *noahwaybabes*, okay, I'm not like, delusional. Still a little mad that all these cool videos that I put effort into are basically glorified ads for confused clients who want

46

to check I'm the kind of trans they're expecting. Couldn't afford shit when I was only doing porn. I swear, tricks all need pictures and video before they get it, doesn't matter how many times I say FTM and bonus hole boi and that I have a pussy on my website."

An increase in our popularity in porn cannot be lauded as a win for transmasculine sex workers when so many of us can't turn that popularity into enough money to survive and white able-bodied thin men are uplifted over everyone else. There's a long way to go, as we tackle racism and ableism and fatphobia in the porn industry at large, and this surge in visibility must be used as an avenue to fight for better treatment and better pay.

Submission 6, by Omar

Ring Light On

Omar is an unapologetically brown, fat, disabled non-binary person. They want more trans people to make porn that they enjoy making, for queer audiences rather than just straight ones.

My ring light makes my skin glow. I slide my hands over my thighs, which are covered in dense and wild hair that I no longer shave before filming. I relax without worrying about how my belly looks from the angle the camera is at and spread my legs to play with my strap.

I used to only film solo videos where I fingered myself or used dildos to penetrate myself, then later I made videos where I sucked off other content creators or let them penetrate me. Now I stroke the dildo attached to me because I like how it feels in my hand and the look of a cock between my legs and I don't care if it's marketable. I let the scars on my leg from getting surgery show and I don't cover them any more.

Like this, I feel sexy. I talk to the camera and imagine the last person I slept with, telling them to ride me. The pleasure is real when I grind up against the base of the strap and moan over it. Transitioning has lost me a lot of subscribers and it's also freed me to make the kind of porn for others that I would want to stumble on myself. I want to watch porn with people in it who are feeling real pleasure and getting off in front of my eyes and that's what I give my fans.

I'll keep making porn as long as anyone's watching. I started for the money but I continue for the trans men and other non-binary people who tell me that finding videos like mine makes them accept their bodies more. Any kind of person could end up seeing my clips on Pornhub or could sign up to my Fansly, but I'm having T4T dreams when I thrust my strap into a fleshlight for a video. Cis people are welcome to be quiet witnesses to my orgasms.

I jerk off the same as I would without a camera there. I'm earning money for something I would do on a daily basis with or without the money.

Custom orders come in, from people who find me on tube sites or see my nudes on Reddit and my lewds on Tumblr and decide to subscribe. They ask me to jiggle my stomach and I feel sexier than ever. One asks me to film a video riding a dildo stuck to my shower wall, which I can't do because of my disability, and I explain the kinds of things I can and can't manage. I'm not ashamed to be open with my fans about being disabled and I've built a group of fans who are understanding. Reclaiming my sexuality from people who want to call me disgusting and to show someone like myself feeling pleasure are the reasons I do this, not catering to ableists.

Using my body to create pleasure is the best thing I can do with it. All the things my body can't do, all the ways people say my body is wrong or disgusting, and I can still make it feel good and find people who want to watch me make that happen.

There are times I get horny and want to watch someone else get off. Trans people with bodies like mine and bodies that are totally different. I'll keep making my own videos until I have too much choice to know what to do with, and then I'll keep going after that, too. I turn off my ring light after I've filmed a few videos and I get ready to edit them.

Submission 7, by Felix Mufti

Felix Mufti is a scouse activist, performer, writer and chaos-causer who loves to tell his unhinged life stories through rhythm n' rap inspired spoken word, poetry, prose and music.

With a passion for many forms of activism, due to his own lived experience, Felix's heart lies deepest with his fellow Queer communities. Although Felix's values, stories and hopes and dreams of Queerness are firmly rooted in all his artistic work, he takes a much more hands on approach wherever possible.

He dreamed of fancy cars. Fancy cars driving to fancy places with fancy people wearing fancy clothes, eating fancy food and drinking fancy drinks. That's all he ever planned to do. To become fancy. He saw it on the telly and it looked boss. He heard about disposable income. He remembered his mum picking pound coins, 50ps, 20ps, 10ps, 5ps, 2ps and 1ps off the floor. Money was anything but disposable. It was all consuming. Hunger became craving. A craving for fancy things.

He learnt how to use their fancy coffee machines, use their fancy words and keep up with their fancy collaborative working platforms. He could never quite wrap his head round them. Who wins when making a virtual mind map? Still, he colour-coded it, correctly sized all his text boxes and pulled all the arrows to the right length. He carefully noted down his thoughts, arranged them succinctly and clearly, until they believed he was fancy too.

He became fancier, working his way up the fancy ladder they dangled above his desk. Oh, how his bones ached to climb. They invited him to fancy dinners and he learnt how to hold his knife, cut his food up and how much wine to drink. Money became disposable. He didn't move out of his mother's house, he bought it for them and made it fancy. He hired professionals with fancy equipment to clear the mould that had been rotting their insides and suffocating their lungs his whole life. It took them a day. He bought the fanciest white paint he could and hid their yellowed walls. His mother had always wanted a chandelier, so he bought her one for her birthday. The fanciest one he could find. No longer needing to pick the change from the floor, she sat for hours, staring at the way it reflected and refracted light into every crevice of their freshly painted walls.

He realized he had officially become fancy when his biggest problem was his favourite coffee shop stopped taking American Express. They always recommended coffee that was too bitter anyway, too strong, too fancy.

Years, nearly a decade, had passed, but he was too busy being fancy to realize. He never really considered love but his mum wanted grandkids. She hated living in a fancy, empty house.

He watched porn. A lot of it. All different types. All different bodies fucking, merging, melting, pulsating, gaping. It wasn't enough for him to watch people have sex anymore. It needed to be taboo, it needed to be violent, it needed to be dirty. He needed to sit in his fancy, waterfall shower after to be cleansed. He didn't turn incognito mode on. There was no one to hide his history from. His phone knew what he needed before he did. The thought of sex workers had never appealed to him before, he never understood why someone would pay for something you could get for free. He wasn't getting anything for free.

An advert popped up, one of the usual ones for a camming website. Instead of skipping, he watched.

I, on the other hand, have never been fancy. Nor have I wanted to be. I have always been happily tacky. Brassy, never classy. Big, long pink XXL acrylic nails. Massive, full-volume Mink Russian Eyelashes. Huge, velour pink tapestries adorning my walls. Everything has always looked empty and bare to me unless decorated with rhinestones, glitter and bows.

He never looked at anything for long. No time to be wasted. When he saw my advert, he stared. His brain tried to piece me together.

My agency had wanted to brand itself as the go-to diverse camming site so planned a huge campaign starring me to run on all the major porn sites.

They paid for me to have my hair and makeup done, my big brown curls perfectly flowing down my shoulders and stacked on my head, each one finger curled, intentional as an awaiting game of Jenga. My lash girl came down to make sure my set was fluffy and inviting, a few pink sparkly lashes on the ends for the occasion. My nail girl came down to make sure there wasn't a rhinestone out of place. They were my favourite set to date, Hello Kitty decals and gems jumping off them, glittering and catching light with every minor hand movement. My toes painted their usual pristine white. I had a spray tan a few days before and there wasn't a patch of my hairy, tattooed body that wasn't golden brown. Me and my favourite make-up artist had been sending Pinterest boards back and forth for weeks. We settled on a sparkly pink chrome eyeshadow for my lids, black wings of liner meticulously curling up my temples. My lips were overlined with a mocha colour, filled in with a gorgeous, rich sparkling gloss. My base was glowy, highlighter and blush stretching up my cheeks and my freckles individually relined with a brown eyeliner pencil. I felt beautiful. Enough to make anyone's sexuality be me.

We decided to go with the brief 'all fur coat, no knickers.' (Adjective, UK, idiomatic, derogatory: Having a superficially positive appearance that is belied by the reality, e.g. superficially elegant and beautiful but actually common.)

Very tongue in cheek. I swallowed myself in my pink (obviously) fluffy coat. I put on my favourite pair of clear 7-inch Pleasers and positioned myself on my bed. The agency had hired a full camera crew to come to my bedroom. A studio wasn't necessary. The point of camming is that it feels personal, like viewers having a front-row seat to your most intimate moments. They set up warm lighting to compliment my skin tone and I sat back on my Bratz bed sheets, completely naked apart from the fur coat. I opened my legs wide and began to play with my hairy pussy. It wasn't reading well on the camera so we added some lube to give it a wetter effect. I moaned and whimpered, begging the camera to 'come play with me,' telling it that I was 'so lonely in my bed' and that I 'need someone to come stretch out my tight, little hole.' It was an oscar-worthy performance. I got the footage back and couldn't have been happier. I looked sexy, free, confident. I told them to run the advert. It wasn't long before I had my regulars texting me to ask when I was next free, telling me I looked great and that the advert had popped up on their phone. My weekly cam viewers skyrocketed. I was struggling to keep on top of my interactions in the chat, which only made them shower me with more virtual gifts.

I never noticed when he first entered my chat. There were so many interchanging screen names, I couldn't keep on top of them. There seemed to be hundreds of 'Hung and Horny's and thousands of 'Big Daddy's. I always had a talent for remembering my regulars, keeping on top of all their kinks and fetishes, different motifs they liked to hear me moan. I knew the ones that liked the vibrating rabbit dildo, the ones that liked squirting, the ones that liked the fluffy tail butt plugs, Now, they were all blurring into one. One big, sexually frustrated, invisible, cyber voyeur. Watching, pulsating, throbbing.

His days became consumed with watching me or waiting for me to come back online. His new promotion meant he had his own office and he utilized it by rubbing his cock impatiently under the desk. Waiting, anticipating, fantasizing.

Eventually, it became enough. He paid to privately message me and asked if I would meet. I asked where he was based – about a 4 hour drive away. He told me he would send a fancy car to his favourite, fancy hotel. He agreed to pay me a fancy amount and we arranged it for the next weekend.

I got ready as I usually do. With my recent pay rise, I could treat myself properly. Fresh sets of nails, nothing too extravagant, just a pink, sparkly french tip and my usual white toes. Ten minutes on the sunbeds this time. I didn't want to turn a hotel's white sheets green with tan. My curls stacked on my head. My favourite Dior lip gloss. With the long drive, there was no point in doing a full face of makeup. The streetlights blurred themselves into one as I unfocused my eyes out the window of the backseat, ignoring the driver's weak attempts at flirting. I seduce for a living; it's going to take more than compliments. He didn't complain about my relentless puffing on my Gummy Bear vape though, so I entertained it.

I turned up to the Park Plaza London Embankment, its big glass walls towering over me. Looming. Waiting. Reflecting. He must have been tracking my car. He arrived on cue. He parked his fancy car on double yellows outside the hotel. Guess paying a ticket is worth that entrance. I don't know much about cars but I know it looked expensive. 'You're wearing the coat,' he said, pointing towards my consuming, pink fluffy coat. My uniform. 'I am.' He nodded. 'You're smaller than I expected.' I nodded. 'Is that a problem?' 'The Opposite.'

He suddenly became very aware of the publicity of our meeting. He asked me to wait outside while he checked in and I waited to be told the room number. I went up in the lift to the top floor. I knocked, my nails digging into my palms. Before the heavy door even opened, he told me 'I've been thinking about you a lot.' I tell him I tend to have that effect on people and he deflated. The room was gorgeous. One of the walls was a huge window showcasing the whole of London. Night time was rapidly approaching and I watched as lights began to sprinkle the view.

All his texts had been very vivid descriptions of what he was going to do to me, graphic details of sex acts I wasn't sure were logistically possible. Closing the space between us had flatted his imagination. We were left silent on the edge of the bed. He paid me upfront. He knew I wouldn't leave. With nowhere to go, just my wide eyes and dreams. I tried to put my hand on his leg, not even as an advance but a comfort. 'I'm so sorry. I fear I've completely wasted your time.' He began to stand up and pack his things away. 'We don't have to fuck if you don't want to. This is a nice room. We can order room service, put a movie on. Just chill?' I say, upholding my best customer service.

We ordered pizza and he ate it with a knife and fork.

This began to happen regularly. Him booking me. The same hotel. No sex. Just sitting, chatting, sharing. He'd tell me how he has so much to spare, he doesn't know what to do with it. I'd tell him I'd always felt spare and I didn't know what to do with myself.

We ordered pizza again. He ate it with his hands and he let the sauce drip down his chin and carried on talking before wiping it off. His shoulders were relaxing, he wasn't hanging up his shirts when taking them off, and his wrists were limping.

That was the last time I saw him.

I still couldn't keep up with my cam viewers. They had decreased since the peak of the advert but I'd built up a reliable base.

I received a private message. Then another. Then another. Then another. I knew exactly who it was before I even read the first word.

'There is never enough hours to spend time with how I feel.
You have burst my wounds open,
I'm scared they will heal.

I know you keep my fate,
wrapped tight in your pocket,
I'll spend a lifetime even asking you to unlock
it.

You are haunting, unwavering, cut me to the
bone,
I have spent my whole life trying to make a
home.

With your in addition it will never feel whole.
I shake in your presence,
yet quiver without.
I'm scared by my dreams, pray for terrors and
shouts.

I must bid farewell to the man of my dreams
I will continue to see you in my make believe.'

He sent me a sum of money. I counted the zeros a few times. I never heard from him again. My fancy man.

Submission 8, by Julian Yang

Thoughts from an Asian Bottom: Why Sex and Gender Can Never Be Fully Separated from Race

Julian Yang (he/she/they) is a British-Born Chinese social anthropologist and full service sex worker. He works as a professional lover and pleasure provider in boy-mode, girl-mode, and everything in between, delivering sensual massages to all who need his touch. He's looking to enter the porn world as a t-boy Nigella Lawson, and make naughty cooking tutorials as Dim Sum Danny *(call him if you can make this happen!)*

Although I've only been doing sex work for a year, my experiences with clients on the job and my time as a slut in London's queer and closeted sex spaces have helped me realise a lot. The most notable thing I've noticed is how the way one is gendered (and sexed) is connected to how one is racialised by others.

This essay argues that neither sex nor gender can be considered independently from the matter of racialisation, especially in the realm of carnal desire. I offer an auto-ethnographic reflection on my gender reassignment journey and lived experience of sex work, as a case study to understand the connections between these themes which draws on literature that synthesises queer theory with critical studies in race and ethnicity. I use this to move beyond the mere acknowledgement that historically the sociocultural formation of sex and gender categories occurred parallel to the development of racial thinking and white supremacy. Many of us are well aware that the reason people box us in as "too masculine", "too feminine", "not masculine enough" or "not feminine enough" is because of racism.

Rather, we will take a closer look at the many consequences of this history in our present lives, by evaluating the contemporary figure of the "Asian Bottom" discussed by Nguyen (2024) in "A View From The Bottom: Asian American Masculinity and Sexual Representation."

Where 'Race' comes into defining 'Sex' and 'Gender'

There are many conceptual hurdles to watch out for when thinking about the links between sex, gender and race.

Firstly, the challenge of defining sex and gender often appears in the colloquial conflation of the two. In everyday conversation they are linguistically interchangeable, e.g. boys are thought of as male and girls as female. The extent to which they are differentiated in contemporary layman's terms is that sex is biologically known and gender is mentally felt. In other words, one's body is a physical object and one's mind is an interior possession. This mind-body distinction originates from Cartesian dualism (Thibaut 2018)[5]. It carries through to so-called 'progressive' discourse in modern neoliberal formulations of identity politics, and is used to delegitimise the existence of transgender individuals – especially those who have not medically transitioned.

Secondly, it is essential to recognise that such dualistic thinking, which places legitimacy in the physical attributes of someone's body rather than their mind, relies on the measurement of physiognomy. Because gender is not something we can choose to code, the "performativity" of it, as Butler (1990)[6] discussed, relies on social norms that were generated beyond our will. The more one is deemed to possess certain traits associated with a particular gender, the more boxes they tick in blue or pink zones, the more securely they are placed in the minds of binary thinkers as mono-gender. Though Hesse (2007: 658)[7] was speaking predominantly on the realities of "racialized modernity", this boxed logic is because "concepts and categories are inherited in traditions… consecrated as the heritage of thought…the recognized or legitimated lineage of thinking, exerts a powerful conventional presence on conceptual formations".

A broad range of literature from sociology to anthropology shows that the "common sense" way we think about sex and gender is linked to how we have

5   Thibaut, F. 2018. The mind-body Cartesian dualism and psychiatry. Dialogues in Clinical Neuroscience 20, 3.

6   Butler, J. 1990. Gender Trouble: Feminism and the Subversion of Identity. New York: Routledge.

7   Hesse, B. 2007. Racialized modernity: An analytics of white mythologies. Ethnic and Racial Studies 30, 643–663.

come to understand race (Lawrence 1982: 45)[8]. It is more than the assumption that prejudice is an inevitable part of human nature. Our common sense manner of discussing these three themes of categorisation is derived from ideological roots. The rules of gender hegemony were formed in conjunction with racialized modernity and white mythologies (Hesse, 2007), leaving sexologists in Western societies to believe that cultures with greater differentiation between men and women signified better-evolved civilizations (Markowitz, 2001)[9]. This is a key contribution of critical race scholarship, demonstrating the gender binary as a colonial import; the recognition that we are being held to ideals thought to be embodied by the white male and female.

"The fear that society is falling apart at the seams" has spurred on reductive modes of thinking in an attempt to preserve cultural norms (Lawrence 1982: 45). We can hear it in the way bodies are policed; big, small, short, or tall. We see it in the lines drawn by cis-normative society; that equate gender to genitalia. The significance of this logic shines through in racialised discussions about 'biological sex' too, particularly surrounding primary or secondary sex characteristics, including penis size, vaginal 'tightness', breast size, facial or body hair, vocal pitch, and bone size. This plots us on a graph of desirability depending on our aesthetic value, which brings me to the main focus of this essay: where we are plotted by other people and why.

---

8   Lawrence, E. 1982. Empire Strikes Back; Race And Racism In 70'S Britain. Abingdon: Routledge.
9   Markowitz, S. 2001. Pelvic Politics: Sexual Dimorphism and Racial Difference. Signs 26, 389–414

Discovering Othered Figures in Sexual Pop Culture

If you've spent any amount of time in the sex work industry, or even just tried your hand at swimming in a digital dating pool, you'll understand the pressure of having to market yourself among a sea of fellow eligible fish. You find ways to stand out by presenting your genuine authentic self, whilst tapping a few bubble-shaped labels that feel tolerable enough to describe you.

"Am I a twink or a twunk? I'd say I'm muscular. Let's go with condoms-only. Kissing. Rigger not rope-bunny. Dominant-leaning switch. ENM... oh yes, means ethical non-monogamy... or am I just poly?".

Before you know it, the site or app then asks the dreaded question: "Nationality/Ethnicity". One hesitates what to put down.

Each race and gender combination will trigger a resulting fetish to be put on us.

I learned this early on. I found porn online when I was underage, after I accidentally came across the Babestation channel by pressing the biggest three-digit numbers I could fathom on the wonky foot-shaped 2007 Sky remote. My parents' English wasn't good enough to figure out how to turn on Parental Control settings on our TV or WiFi to block adult content, so I picked up the vocabulary needed to search for smut on Google rather quickly. I was led to a book of pages on xHamster from clicking on "A" for Asian, catching glimpses of unrecognisable strangers to fan-cut clips of celebrities like Lucy Liu and Michelle Yeoh. It didn't take me long to figure out that the actors who looked most like me at the time, Yellow[10] women, played very specific characters. They were either obedient, child-like submissives whose whimpers were dialled to a pre-pubescent timbre, or futuristic, sadistically-threatening assassins with swords. Straight black hair. Slim as hell. Both found in media intended to arouse a Western gaze and an appetite for something exotic.

Feeling like I had watched enough content of Yellow (cisgender) women, I moved on to browsing other films in the suggestion column. Other colour and gender configurations. What began as a curious horny exploration of places that would show me more boobs than pay-per-view BabeStation turned into a spiralling fascination with the way people were being sorted sexually. I came to view simple nudity and stayed to investigate the perversions of audiences that I felt committed to sussing out. I thought to myself: Who else is seeing this? My classmates? My teachers? The postman? Neighbourhood policeman? Corner shop bossman?

A theory is posited by bell hooks that such a desire for "Eating the Other" is what fuels the demand and creation of "content to 'exploit' white eroticization of black bodies" (hooks, 1992: 63)[11]. In its most dehumanising forms, she explains that sexual iconography depicting Black men can be heavily "phallocentric" reducing them to a mere body part (ibid: 95) whereas depictions of Black women place them

---

10 I don't censor the word Yellow because it has its uses. Like with other slurs that I have been called, such as tranny, I find a level of utility comes with reclaiming it to describe a political identity.

11 hooks, bell 1992. Black looks: race and representation. New York: Routledge.

either in the category of "mammy or slut, and occasionally a combination of the two" (ibid: 72). She says that this comes alongside a fantasy to "fuck as many girls" from each "racial/ethnic group" as possible "to leave behind white 'innocence' and enter the world of 'experience'" (ibid: 23).

This lines up with what I observed as a young internet user, in addition to the ostracising absence of Yellow male representation on my computer screen. Off the top of my head, my first impression of sexual Yellow masculinity were the creepy uncle characters in Japanese hentai. And though I do not wish to push my mum under the bus, she often described East Asian men as sexless because of her resentment towards my father's stark asexuality. I must admit, it wasn't until I was forced to consider existing as a Yellow man myself that I began to develop reflections about Asian masculinity on a deeper level than the stereotypes I had internalised from wider society. I could no longer run from confronting my own lack of reflexivity when building my profiles on Tinder, Feeld, Grindr, Squirt, and Adultwork and the machine/its users asked for answers on my ethnic identity.

Being an Asian Bottom

To illustrate my reflections, I want to tell the story of not just my first (dyke) slut era but my subsequent (twink) slut renaissance, and how sex work has brought me into richer self-actualisation.

I have always been attracted to men. To be truthful, I did not deem myself to be male enough to engage in physical intimacy with them until I started testosterone – that is, for the sex to 'count as gay and not straight'. The images I'd seen of Yellow femmes in sexual media, and the way they were treated as a result of their gender was a dysphoria-inducing sight. So, prior to HRT kicking in, I presented as a masc lesbian and had sex with as many women as I could to accrue a self-perceived status of possessing sexual capital. Becoming more secure in my gender identity, my subsequent sexual orientation, and exploring the gay cruising scene occurred around the same period of time. I started HRT at the end of November 2021, and downloaded Grindr a month later at the peak of my first wave of "bottom growth" and the first of many libido spikes. When I got a bit braver, I joined Squirt.com, a site that lists cruising locations across London, from public bathrooms to famed al-fresco-fucking parks such as Hampstead Heath.

Among the 4x3 block of "headless torso pictures" (Nguyen 2024: 28) on my Grindr homepage saying "dom bull top", "sub slut bottom", I was an anomaly. My thumbs hovered over the letters on my phone screen. "FTM Dom Bottom", I tap.

The thought of doing sex work occurred to me long before I transitioned. A mix of hypersexuality, high tolerance for the strangeness of humanity, and possessing a caregiving, service-prone nature made me well-suited for it. Before I started charging, I went on a free for hot guys fucking spree to prepare my pussy for handling bio-penises. The strapons I had run-ins with during my dyke era never had such variation in turgidness. I wanted to learn how to ride dick well; perform pro-level fellatio I could be proud to charge money for, and that I did. Skills? Sorted. But I got stuck on my personal branding. During the time I spent as a young porn explorer, I came across a bounty of MTF content. Scattered amidst the straight, gay, and lesbian sections, it seemed well-embraced by commenters. There was even a subcategory for "Asian chicks with dicks" that awoke intense penis envy within me. However, there were no pornos showing FTMs, or Asian mascs, let alone Asian FTMs. Though representation of "guys with pussies" has risen greatly since the days of Buck Angel, with new stars on the rise like NoahWayBabe and ApolloMoon, I was still worried about the lack of visibility and awareness of transmasculine existence.

To combat this, and mark my spot as a recognisable hooker despite my rarity, I put on masks that put me in charge of how others saw me. Sex and consent in vanilla/civ life is often discussed as something to be kept clean and clear-cut. However, when you're racialized in sex work, or just a minoritised person in the neoliberal sexual marketplace, there is always the potential that those we consent to having sex with couple be engaging in quiet mental race play. For my sex work practice, I had to accept this as a constant occupational hazard. Fortunately, I've found my own ways of compartmentalising such tasking emotional and affective labour – so I can still produce the right fantasy that will elicit the most lucrative response from my clients.

Nguyen (2014) talks about this strategy called "yellow yellowface", when Asian American performers are in situations where they might act out stereotypical characters and find room for subversion in it. I've been doing that since I was little. Explaining ingredients and dishes to the ignorant but curious diners that I grew up serving in my family's Chinese restaurant prepared me perfectly for explaining my appeal to clients who have never had the pleasure of fucking a guy like me. If you can convince white geezers to try tofu and wonton soup, you can get a gold-star gay man with a phobia of vaginas to see why your warm puss and 3-year grown t-dick are also delicious.

Thus, choosing to survive and live in the realms of hedonism meant I turned to capitalising on the parts of myself that I knew could be reliably eroticised and leaned into it.

If clients have a taste for "eating the Other" (hooks 1992), then fuck it – I'll make myself look like dim sum.

Bibliography and References:

Butler, J. 1990. Gender Trouble: Feminism and the Subversion of Identity. New York: Routledge.

C. Riley Snorton 2017. Black on Both Sides. U of Minnesota Press.

Hall, K. F. 2018. Things of Darkness: Economies of Race and Gender in Early Modern England. Ithaca, NY: Cornell University Press.

Hesse, B. 2007. Racialized modernity: An analytics of white mythologies. Ethnic and Racial Studies 30, 643–663.

hooks, bell 1992. Black looks: race and representation. New York: Routledge.

Lawrence, E. 1982. Empire Strikes Back; Race And Racism In 70'S Britain. Abingdon: Routledge.

Markowitz, S. 2001. Pelvic Politics: Sexual Dimorphism and Racial Difference. Signs 26, 389–414 (available online: https://www.jstor.org/stable/3175447, accessed 7 July 2024).

Nguyen, T. H. 2014. A view from the bottom : Asian American masculinity and sexual representation. Durham: Duke University Press.

Thibaut, F. 2018. The mind-body Cartesian dualism and psychiatry. Dialogues in Clinical Neuroscience 20, 3 (available on-line: https://www.ncbi.nlm.nih.gov/pmc/articles/PMC601604 7/, accessed).

Valentine, D. 2007. Imagining Transgender. Duke University Press.

Chapter 3: Transphobic Violence Against Transmasculine Sex Workers

Transphobic violence is a plague which shortens trans peoples' lives or takes them away, limiting our joy and bringing us immense pain as individuals and as a community. Trans sex workers in particular are highly likely to be targeted for extreme kinds of transphobic violence, including sexual abuse. This is evident to me from speaking to multitudes of other trans people, however we lack good statistics covering the issue and we cannot rely solely on anecdotes.

When it comes to trans men and transmasculine non-binary people who do sex work, finding the little data that exists is difficult because often the label "trans sex worker" is employed to refer exclusively to transfeminine people selling sex. Reliable research about transfeminine sex workers is by no means easy to find in the first place, as sex workers tend to avoid being studied when we can out of fear of state intervention in our lives and transfeminine people have multiple reasons to be fearful of surveillance. Ultimately, transmasculine people are left to pick through the few studies that exist searching for footnotes or survey answers that are broken down into demographics.

Academics and researchers will often discuss the high rate of violence against trans sex workers and expect the listener to assume that the sex workers being discussed are trans women. Well-meaning people will echo their statements and assumptions and it becomes even harder to separate the information. Trans women who do sex work are the population who are rendered the most visible and who are vilified in the media the most often. They are depicted as caricatures of themselves within fiction where their suffering is the punchline of a joke, and real transfeminine sex workers are made into subjects of ridicule or are interviewed for shock value. Contrasting this, there is a lack of cultural awareness of trans men doing sex work at all, particularly when we are speaking about full service sex work (selling sex in-person). Researchers fail to consider us and the research continues to be vague or to study only certain groups of trans people.

The National Transgender Discrimination Survey, a USA-based study conducted in 2011, found that 7% of 'FtM' respondents reported having engaged in sex work as part of the underground economy[12]. The same survey recorded that 'MtF' respondents engaged in sex work at over twice that rate, with 15% of them reporting it. 6,450 study participants were interviewed to gain this information, of whom 28% were categorized as FtM. These numbers encompassed only the trans people who strongly identified with the binary language presented to them. 14% of all the respondents were

12 National Transgender Discrimination Survey: Full Report – page 64.

grouped into the "gender non-conforming" category, which consisted of 78% of participants identifying as "on the female-to-male spectrum". Essentially, most of the gender non-conforming category was transmasculine. Of the gender non-conforming group, 10% reported engaging in sex work.

Although the National Transgender Discrimination Survey breaks down how much more likely trans sex workers are to be homeless or HIV+ or to attempt suicide, as well as including references to mistreatment whilst doing sex work as being a cause of drinking and drug issues among sex workers, it does not provide statistics on the rate of violence experienced by trans sex workers. We are left to make assumptions and extrapolate from the little information given to us.

I wish I could share studies with representative samples of the trans population that would give us good numbers, to have undeniable proof that transmasculine sex workers face a heightened risk of assault compared to non sex workers or to cis sex workers. We can infer that the rate of violence is high, combining the knowledge that transmasculine people are very likely to be assaulted[13] and that sex workers are at a higher risk of violence compared to non sex workers[14]. Nevertheless, I don't want to infer, I want to know, because this guesswork doesn't tell us how much whorephobia and transphobia towards transmasculine people might amplify each other.

---

13 *The Report of the 2015 US Transgender Survey* – pages 133, 134, 205.

14 Deering KN, Amin A, Shoveller J, Nesbitt A, Garcia-Moreno C, Duff P, Argento E, Shannon K. *A systematic review of the correlates of violence against sex workers*. Am J Public Health. 2014 May.

Evidence of the quantity of transmasculine sex workers who are experiencing assault and harassment allows advocates for our well-being to prove the need for our inclusion in sex worker support services. Charities struggle enough to get the money to support sex workers when they do have reports and data to demonstrate the level of risk – without numbers to show to their funders, we go ignored.

As an under-studied population, we also tend to end up being viewed more like a homogenous mass than as individuals. Any context where we are included is likely to be the sole instance of transmasculine sex worker representation that much of the audience has ever seen. Instances where transmasculine sex workers *are* invited to speak will include predominately those who are in positions of relative privilege and experience less assault, and the audience absorbs their accounts as a sort of baseline.

Small groups of workers who aim to share their experiences and fill in the gaps themselves are still likely to be limited, doing so with their personal friends which leads to a continued lack of diversity among the people whose accounts we can learn about. Films like *Shinjuku Boys*[15] give us amazing insight, but interviews with three transmasculine Japanese sex workers whose clients are women doesn't show us anything close to a representative experience, nor should we expect it to! The scope is too narrow.

Trans people in the US who are Black and Black multiethnic are overrepresented in sex work[16], unsurprisingly due to the discrimination they face, yet

15 *Shinjuku Boys*, 1995, by Kim Longinotto and Jano Williams.
16 *Meaningful Work: Transgender Experiences in the Sex Trade*, December 2015 – page 4.

details about the transmasculine contingent are hard to come by and it is difficult to ascertain information on how much violence they experience. Given how much more violence Black sex workers face in the US in general, it follows that the risk to Black transmasculine Americans in sex work will also be high, but the lack of an ability to quantify the risk leads to additional issues. Since the voices being heard are often white transmasculine sex workers, when transmasculine sex workers have the opportunity to speak at all, advice provided by us about the likelihood of experiencing abuse (based on personal experience) could be off by an order of magnitude.

Whenever I speak to trans men and transmasculine non-binary people who are interested in starting sex work, their fears include concerns that they will be sexually assaulted by clients in-person or stalked and attacked by customers or people from their personal life who find them online. Two separate transmasculine former sex workers I interviewed, who both sold porn on subscription sites, informed me that their nudes were accidentally stumbled upon by friends and they feared violent reactions. The worker who had been selling sexual content for longest said, "It was such a sudden thing, the subreddits for trans guy porn getting popular. One day there was zero chance of anyone I knew seeing the teasers I posted, the next I was getting texts about my bare ass showing up on my friends' home pages. It was a scary time, especially because a couple of my ex-friends were aggressive about it and mad that they'd seen me like that."

Making reassurances that online-only sex work is totally safe would be disingenuous, and the same is true of in-person activities. We must work from the assumption that the danger is there, planning around it, because the alternative is to let generations of transmasculine sex workers suffer and struggle while someone else gathers data. I'm pleased every time I hear from a transmasculine worker who adores their work and never deals with any trouble, but I'm wary and cognizant of how necessary it is to take precautions. I am aware of how much worse my experience would be if not for the precautions I do take, and how much I have been protected because I have not had to deal with racism or ableism targeted at me.

Abuse of transmasculine sex workers often occurs in relation to our transness, rather than our transness solely contributing to the conditions that make us into targets for abuse (poverty due to employment discrimination or being kicked out of home, a lack of appropriate sex education, etc.) Our transness is a trait which adds to how often we are assaulted, on top of other things we might be targeted for like disability or ethnicity or sexuality. Hence, access to transition may be used as a bargaining chip to keep us with an abusive partner, as sex work tends not to be a stable income and transition services are expensive. Who ends up in this difficult position will be a matter of socio-economic status, which will be influenced by the other ways the transmasculine sex worker is marginalized, and being trans then acts as the method of trapping the sex worker so that they cannot escape the violence.

Clients may take their frustrations about their sexuality out on us, using us as a punching bag because our transness renders us less human or deserving of compassion to them, or experience unexpected disgust upon seeing us naked. Transphobia is pervasive and thus so are the reasons that someone might engage in transphobic violence against us.

Radical feminists are not the only group with a strong awareness that the majority of sex workers are women; clients are well aware that it is overwhelmingly women who are paid for sexual services. For this reason, attacks against transmasculine sex workers often include an element of feminization which is tied to our work. We may be degraded as we are assaulted, with the insistence that we are actually women because we would never choose to sell sexual services otherwise. On other occasions, clients might insist that we should tolerate certain forms of abuse on the basis that a cis man in our position would consent to the same acts – a lie which plays into homophobic stereotypes and the disturbing rhetoric which claims men cannot be raped.

Corrective rape is also employed against transmasculine sex workers, by clients of in-person sex workers as well as the partners or colleagues or fans of those whose work takes place online. The attempted correction is two-fold: it seeks to teach us our supposed place as *women*, and it seeks to teach us not to be *whores*. We are expected to learn that the kind of sex we can expect as men and non-binary people will be devoid of the care that women can expect, although this is certainly a fabrication because such rapists do not treat women well either, and that selling sex means choosing to be vulnerable to sexual abuse. Assaults of this nature were the cause for many of the former sex workers I spoke with to end up homeless or in serious debt, because they could no longer continue to sell sex afterwards.

Beliefs about gender, violence and sexual assault can impact how trauma from sexual abuse is processed. Men are not immune to rape and are equally traumatized by it when it happens to them, yet societal stigma carries an expectation that they should not be. The manifestation of this stigma in cis men is evident in their reticence to speak about instances of being assaulted, their jokes brushing it off, and their difficulty processing it. Trans men and transmasculine people may experience these same effects in the aftermath of an assault, with the likely addition of significant dysphoria because of the associations made between being assaulted and being feminine. That these associations are not reasonable does not change the way the mind processes the memory, and how PTSD triggers may manifest and interact with gender dysphoria.

In addition to the more clear-cut instances of rape or other physical assaults, there are also violations of boundaries which tend to be viewed differently by people who experience them often than by those who do not. Make no mistake, these consent violations undeniably meet the definition of sexual assault; they just aren't always viewed as assault by those who are experiencing them, or aren't experienced as being serious violations when compared to other instances of rape.

A trans man I interviewed told me, upon being asked about how often he'd been assaulted, "Counting every time a guy has put his fingers in my ass without asking, I've been assaulted dozens of times. We're down to a dozen if we only count the times they keep trying to finger me or stick their dicks in after I've told them no. I say three times, if someone outright asks how many times I've been raped." I found that I related to his experience, as someone who often struggles to quantify how many times I have been assaulted. It is difficult to

78

know where to place the line, in accordance with what the other person is imagining when they ask the question. If we assume that transmasculine people are more likely to be assaulted both because we are trans and because we are sex workers, we must also recognize that these more frequent assaults will cause us to under-report the total number of times we have been harmed. Not to mention that some of us will simply not be able to remember the total number of times we have been sexually assaulted or harassed.

My personal friends cannot be used as representatives for the average experience of transmasculine sex workers, but a large portion of those I know well have confided in me that they have experienced assault. Almost all of those who have experienced it have had it occur multiple times, before and after transitioning, at the hands of partners and clients and family and police alike. The same has been true of those I have interviewed, who I have questioned on the subject. Although many answer that they have not been assaulted, like one non-binary respondent to a survey I conducted, these answers come with caveats. "I've been lucky – no-one has ever touched me in a way I didn't want while whoring, and my clients listen to my instructions. Not that I see that many – I'm super picky. Pretty much all the other transmascs I known in this industry have been harmed at some point, though, so I know how privileged I am. It's because of their advice that I think I've avoided it for so long."

Another common anecdote about experiences of violence that I have noticed recurring in my interviews with other transmasculine sex workers has been that clients become aggressive when they mistakenly believe we are trans women. I have had this experience myself, while working in a brothel early into my medical transition, and had not realized at the time that it was so seemingly widespread. It is easy to forget how little the average person knows about trans bodies or transition care, as a trans person or ally who is well-versed in the effects of HRT and surgery, but clients can easily become confused when faced with someone who has atypical sexual characteristics.

Regarding his experiencing being attacked because he was believed to be a trans woman, an intersex sex worker told me, "My vulva's always looked different, because I'm intersex and had an operation when I was still a kid to make it look more typical. I have a couple of scars. Johns never commented on it before I got on T, then when I got hairy and my voice dropped and I was still cis for pay I started getting suspicious questions and comments. The johns got rougher and I thought I was imagining it. I thought they suspected that I'm a trans man. Wasn't 'till a trick started ranting about how I'd tricked him and hitting me that I realized he thought I was a trans woman." These kinds of assaults are the result of transmisogynistic ideas held by clients, but they directly impact us because the transphobic bigotry they hold includes a misunderstanding of how trans bodies work and a hatred for anyone who is gender non-conforming.

Not all attacks by clients or partners or those in our social circles will be sexual in nature, as is the case with some of those mentioned above, yet they are some of the first that people picture because of the nature of our work. The assumption that the violence we face is exclusively sexual in nature is a false belief which does not hold up to scrutiny. Violence faced by transmasculine sex workers varies from rough handling by police during brothel raids to beatings from relatives who think that making trans porn is a stain on the entire family. We are unlikely to be engaging in street sex work whilst openly trans due to the lack of demand, insulating us from certain types of danger though limiting our options for work, but we face elevated levels of danger during indoor work from those who want to target us for being trans.

Detransition is suggested as a solution to the way we are targeted, by transphobic cis people who fail to grasp the trade-off, as is leaving sex work. These ideas, naturally, ignore the financial reasons that people do sex work and the psychological damage done by forcible detransition. Cis speculation also fails to account for the impact of dysphoria (made worse by detransition) on a person's desire to commit acts of self-inflicted violence, thereby not protecting us from it at all. When faced with exclusively bad options, we are not unreasonable for picking the best of them. As one eloquent interviewee put it, "I'd rather have a few clients hit me and get rough and afford top surgery within the year than go unmolested and kill myself in the GIC queue."

Those of us who continue to do sex work, especially whilst advertising ourselves as being transmasculine or claiming to be cis women despite having visible effects from testosterone, generally do so with awareness of the risk we are taking. Our decisions cannot be brushed away under the assumption that we are acting irrationally. Depending on our circumstances, we may consider the risk to be acceptably low and otherwise find the work fits with our lifestyle, and for some of us there is simply no better alternative. Rather than telling us to quit our jobs due to the bigotry of others, compelling the abusers to find other targets instead, the issue must be resolved at its core. Whorephobia and transphobia must be eradicated in their entirety, to make trans sex workers safe.

Submission 9, by Faye

Escape Hatch

Faye is a non-binary former sex worker, current minimum wage worker, and a survivor of sexual violence. They advocate for free housing and therapy for victims of domestic abuse.

[Names have been changed in the piece below to preserve anonymity.]

I didn't come out as non-binary late in life – it was just later than it would have been, if not for my ex. Daniel was straight and he didn't want me to start HRT or look masculine because of how people would view him, used to tell me he wasn't gay and that I should get the idea that I wasn't a woman out of my head, and insisted that his attraction to me was based in me being so inherently feminine. I loved him and I let him convince me that I was mistaken about being trans. His abuse kept me closeted and also led me to becoming a sex worker.

It seems really stupid now, that I didn't realize how controlling Daniel was and leave. I'm sure you can already guess he got a lot worse. By the time we'd been together for a couple of years, he was yelling at me all the time and he'd started to assault me. I didn't think of it as him assaulting me when he did it, which means it's even more important that I use the right words now. I was getting more dysphoric and miserable because I couldn't transition and I resented him, so I didn't want to sleep with him, and so he started to touch me when I was asleep after I refused him sex.

Staying with him wasn't just a product of conditioning or idiocy – I stayed with him partly because he earned a lot more than I did and he paid our rent. My anxiety and depression (and PTSD, made worse by him assaulting me all the time, I know now) kept me from holding down the supermarket jobs I was getting. I called in sick a lot. I'd only last for a couple of months in any job and could never save enough to break up with him and be able to afford my own place.

Daniel actually gave me the idea to start selling sex, to afford to leave him. He watched a lot of porn throughout our whole relationship, hiding it and then telling me that I didn't sleep with him often enough whenever I walked in on him watching it or saw a tab open on his computer. Since talking it through in therapy, I've realized he likely wanted me to be upset over it and start initiating sex more so he'd watch less porn. When that didn't work, he escalated to threatening to find a sex worker to have sex with – in words much less respectful than those. It sparked something.

I wanted to avoid sex with him as much as possible, which made his threats to cheat on me very empty. I hoped he would start paying sex workers and leave me alone. He made the comments often enough that I started to think he was seeing them and still molesting me in my sleep anyway, and I was really angry. Not just angry but also jealous. I was angry and jealous that someone else might be earning money for what I was putting up with for free. They'd be getting way more than me per hour of sex, if I added up all the times he woke me up or pressured me or ignored me saying I wasn't in the mood. I don't know if he really was seeing sex workers, then. I wouldn't be surprised.

In the beginning, I was terrified of getting caught selling sex and what Daniel would do. I did a lot of internet searching until I found an ad for escorts to work in a flat, that said I didn't need to have any experience. I want to kick myself for not putting up my own ads and working for myself then, but I didn't know any better. The brothel manager taught me a lot about the websites to advertise on and how they worked and he gave me a phone. I worked on a schedule, on days Daniel worked late, waiting for the other shoe to drop. I always felt like I was ten seconds from getting caught.

I know I'm really lucky in this way, and I'm not bragging when I say this but I just want to explain why someone who was raped and traumatized would trade an abusive boyfriend for working in an illegal brothel for a manager who took 40% of my money – no client has ever made me feel as bad during sex as Daniel did. Clients would do things I didn't like or that I told them not to do sometimes, like putting fingers in places I told them were off-limits, but I never had that ice cold feeling of violation. Once I was used to it, I knew it was a job I could keep doing even with my anxiety and depression.

We broke up and Daniel never found out, as far as I know. Our conversations after I ended things were all over text, long paragraphs from him about how I'd come back because I couldn't keep a job and no-one else would put up with me, and I blocked him after a few weeks of it. I worked at the flat until I found a supermarket job again and this time I kept it. It was way less difficult to go to work in the mornings when Daniel hadn't woken me up by assaulting me the night before.

All together, I was only a sex worker for about a year. I did it so that I could leave him. Processing what happened to me made me start to hate all sex, so I got my new job when I started to get triggered while seeing clients, and I've never gone back to it.

Finally, I made new friends and connected with old ones. I told them that I'm trans and I've got an appointment to start medical transition. I hadn't thought about me being non-binary and the sex work as being connected in any important way, except I realize now that without selling sex from that flat I wouldn't be transitioning now. I'd still be with Daniel, not able to imagine leaving because I didn't have the money to stop being in denial about how bad he was for me.

Sex work was a method of escape for me, from an abusive boyfriend and from the dysphoria he trapped me in.

Submission 10, by Mischa

Mischa is a bisexual non-binary sex worker who has been an escort for 2 years. They are now taking a break, looking for other employment so they can recover from their trauma.

Little phrases get stuck in my head sometimes, from clients who say hateful or transphobic stuff to me or lurkers who insult me in forums.

You don't sound too manly, that's good.

Could you still dress up as a woman for me, like in some old lingerie or a skirt or a dress?

She can't be having any luck, I wouldn't fuck her for even half that price when she looks like a hermaphrodite.

When the attention-whoring goes past the actual whoring. They should ban all the profiles with this gender shit on them clogging the site up.

You won't get rid of those tits, will you? I can't imagine you without them.

One phrase has stuck worse than all the others, since a client told me (because I don't offer anal) that I must not be a man because I don't want to get fucked like one. I remember that comment better than I remember him raping me afterwards. I used to think about it almost every time I had sex, even though I didn't have bottom dysphoria about using my front hole for sex before and I'm not a man (though I call myself FTM for work). I would go between feeling like I'm supposed to offer anal to clients since I'm not a woman and being terrified of anyone trying it with me, those words reappearing in my head.

The client definitely targeted me for being trans, it's obvious from what he said. I don't know if being a sex worker was part of why he picked me to rape. I've had sex with more people than all of my trans friends who aren't sex workers too (and huge chunk of my non sex worker trans friends have been raped), so part of me wonders if it's just a numbers game. Was I spinning the wheel on being raped for being trans every time I had sex? The thought that I was giving the wheel extra spins by escorting terrified me.

Actions that were minor annoyances when I first became a sex worker started to be triggers. I'd have clients who were rough with me, who ignored noises of discomfort I made, and I used to feel irritated by their rudeness but be fine otherwise. Any time a man suddenly smacked my backside I'd be terrified he'd decide to do more things without asking. Occasionally they did (up to and including assaults like the first time).

The trauma from being raped made me more vulnerable. I froze up when clients crossed boundaries and didn't tell them to stop. The phrases that were stuck in my head morphed into the idea that being assaulted itself was feminizing. I know that people of all genders get assaulted and that my body and what people do to it doesn't make me a woman, but the truth about that gets knocked out of my head and replaced with my rapist's words every time a client does something I don't like.

I'm not in a position to be able to protect myself from assault, with the way I freeze up any time a client makes me uncomfortable. Dysphoria that was mild before has gotten so extreme that I'm stuck having panic attacks when I'm cleaning myself after sex.

I'm taking a break from sex work because I can't keep going, but I can't actually afford to stop. I don't know if I'll have a choice about going back to it before I've learned to cope. Escorting with pushy and inconsiderate clients makes me dysphoric about being treated like a woman, and nowhere else wants to hire me because I'm trans and have no work experience I can admit to.

For now, I'm working on pulling the most painful phrases out of my head by replacing them with better ones. I tell myself that the parts I use for sex say nothing about my gender. I remind myself that random men aren't an authority on what my gender is (that's mine to determine). I'm just as non-binary as I was before I became an escort.

Chapter 4: The Cost of Medical Transition

Medical transition can have costs for trans sex workers that are not exclusive to the price of surgery or prescriptions or appointments with doctors. Our desirability to clients is impacted by our sex characteristics, therefore so is our income. The removal of breasts, changes to our genitals, or the masculinization that comes with taking testosterone will change whether certain clients are interested in booking transmasculine sex workers at all. Surgeries will put us out of work during the recovery period, leaving us in limbo wondering how much money we may still be capable of earning, depending on the reaction of the client pool to our new bodies.

Affording surgery or HRT is a fantastic incentive for transmasculine people to sell sex. We are discriminated against in employment and earn less than cis people on average, so sex work sometimes becomes our only reasonable option for saving money for something like top surgery or metoidioplasty or phalloplasty. These surgeries can cost tens of thousands of pounds, making them prohibitively expensive for the average person.

The high cost of medical transition is also likely to steer trans people towards higher paid forms of sex work, despite the relative danger. In-person forms of sex work like full service sex work or stripping tend to pay more, compared to online-only options, with the exception of performers who become well-known. For transmasculine people who want to seek masculinizing medical treatment, there is a short window where we can attain our maximum earning potential under the kind of female personas we discussed earlier. In the hopes of making this window as short as possible, transmasculine people may take more risks than we would otherwise like to with the clients we take and the ways we work.

Working whilst claiming to be a cis woman, presenting femininely with a female persona, allows trans sex workers to accumulate the money for HRT and surgery more quickly than if we were openly trans. As we transition, our income typically drops, potentially leaving us stuck at one stage of transition if we did not earn enough money from sex work before we began. To maintain the desired pace to our medical transition, we are forced to make sacrifices and to plan them well in advance.

We might save enough money to afford testosterone and be desperate to take it, but have to hold off on doing so if we hope to afford top surgery in a timely manner. Some of us will make the decision to delay transition until we have saved enough for top surgery, only to be left with the same dilemma about lowering our income and the possibility that we will never afford bottom surgery. There are options in between, to start testosterone and hide it for as long as

91

possible or to film content in bulk and keep selling it when our bodies no longer look the way they did, all involving the same types of risk calculations and their own drawbacks.

Denial is a strong defense mechanism that many trans people find ourselves using, to protect ourselves from the worst of our dysphoria. It can be emotionally easier to deny to ourselves that we are trans than to admit that we are and that we must refrain from coming out or making changes to our bodies because of our circumstances. With the financial struggles that lead many people into sex work irrespective of their transness, there are many trans sex workers who do not yet recognize that they are trans when they start doing the work due to a need for money; some of these sex workers do not allow themselves to accept that they are trans until they are able to afford medical transition, because they know the anguish of waiting longer would be worse than a little more time in denial with clients misgendering them. I have known many sex workers who spent months or years in poverty, only to come out the moment they have built up some savings and rush headfirst into transition as soon as they can. I'm often wistful about how much better off I'd be financially now, if I'd held onto my denial for longer.

At the point where we decide that medical transition is worth the cost, however we arrive at that point, we are forced to omit information when dealing with medical professionals or face additional barriers. Gender therapists will ask us about our sex lives and gender presentation, leaving us to weigh up the likelihood that we would be rejected for treatment if we tell them about our work against our desire to be honest. Any doctor may decide they do not believe we fit the criteria, or that we are lying about our gender identity, if they know we regularly sell sexual services to men who think we're women. We've come a long way since Lou Sullivan pushed for gay trans men to be recognized as men and to have access to medical transition, yet bigotry still persists when it comes to trans people selling sexual services.

Transgender sex workers who begin sex work after they have attained the transition milestones they want will not have to worry about lying to get initial diagnoses and referrals, but they will still face stigma from their doctors. In the current political climate, with constant attacks on trans healthcare continuing, all transmasculine people are at risk of disruptions to their HRT prescriptions, so adding another marginalised identity only increases the danger. Lying continues to be an important safety measure and many of us benefit from keeping our status as sex workers out of our medical records.

Beyond the doctors and therapists we must interact with to gain access to medical transition in ways that are legal, there are yet more medical professionals we interact with as sex workers. Services which exist to provide us with STI tests or resources cater overwhelmingly to women, and our state of medical transition may impact how good the care we receive from these services is. These issues impact us no matter when we started sex work, be it pre-transiton or after beginning HRT and getting surgery. Even the transmasculine people who are uninterested in medically transitioning are not spared, because coming out to a medical professional or being visibly trans will cause them to treat us differently.

Basic care from STI clinics can be impacted by our medical transition. Nurses who administer tests or ask us questions are often not familiar with how our bodies work or the kinds of sex we are capable of having, so they make assumptions and their biases can lead to worse care. When we need access to PrEP, a HIV preventative, we may be given incorrect information about its effectiveness based on the assumption that we use certain parts of our anatomy and have vaginal sex (PrEP takes longer to be effective for vaginal sex than anal sex). Our issues with vaginal atrophy can be overlooked as being the result of seeing so many clients or having so much sex, leading to assumptions that we aren't using enough lube or that the sheer amount of sex is the issue, rather than recognizing the effects a lack of estrogen can have on our genitals.

It is no wonder, given all the issues that can arise for transmasculine sex workers when we seek out medical transition, that there are so many of us who do sex work only prior to our transition and quit afterwards. I was not surprised to hear from one transmasculine sex worker that his retirement was more of a logical conclusion than a choice he made based on preference. "When I dropped to earning barely more than I was spending on ads, after I got top surgery, I realized I had to retire."

The transmasculine sex workers who do continue to do sex work after we transition frequently find that we change the type of sex work we do, moving from brothel work to independent full service sex work or from that to online porn creation, and lower the volume of clients and customers that we interact with. Different stages in transition can require entire re-brands.

To lower the number of trans people who engage in sex work out of desperation, as opposed to making the decision under less pressure, the cost of medical transition needs to be covered by other means. Ending employment discrimination gets us closer, but with the low rate of pay that the average working class person can expect that still won't be enough to mitigate the need for an additional income source to afford medical transition quickly. Transition care, like all vital medical care, must be made free if we wish to remove it as a factor which drives people to sell sex.

Submission 11, by Mx Dagger

An Appointment at Charing Cross

Danny Dagger is a UK based writer, pornogapher, smut peddler and orgasm dealer. They specialise in all things t4t and kinky. When not sex working, they write poetry, crochet hats and live a life happily in servitude to their cat Princess Lunatic.

It's uncomfortably hot as I stand up from my chair in the waiting room and follow the man who has come to summon me. We haven't met before but he has a reputation for being hard on fat trans people and sex workers – I am both. I think I'm prepared, though. I've had a few appointments in this building with various clinicians, psychiatrists and endocrinologists. It definitely doesn't seem as scary as it used to, which is probably the Too Many milligrams of Diazepam I took to stop myself from throwing up on the tube here talking.

We take our seats and he does some clicking about on the computer, before picking up his fountain pen and uncapping it. He is the first person here who takes notes on paper, which he does throughout the course of our meeting. He uses green ink, too. I feel like that's an important detail. I have a feeling he likes using green ink so much that it's the whole reason he takes notes on paper. Alright, I think, I just need a surgery referral. Be sane and stable. Be normal, for fuck's sake. I've previously been denied top surgery; first because I had to be on testosterone for 2 years prior, then because I tried to kill myself. I tried to explain that I wasn't sure if I wanted testosterone at all and that I'd tried to kill myself because I was denied top surgery, but the Gender Clinic rebuffed my attempts to attain those two referrals. Since then, I had been on testosterone for almost two years and built myself a small business. Sure, I'm a sex worker, but it's stable and profitable. Those are the only things that are supposed to matter.

My doctor has other thoughts. He hammers me on details, asking what type of sex work I do and whether it makes me dysphoric. I respond that everything makes me dysphoric and that at least I can be dysphoric indoors on a reasonably comfortable sofa, instead of being on the streets. I wasn't planning on making it a class issue, but I explain that while dysphoria is unpleasant it's present constantly regardless of what I'm doing and is still preferable to hunger and homelessness. I tell him that if he's concerned about my dysphoria then he should refer me for surgery already.

"But hold on," he starts. "If I approve you for surgery, what happens to your business?"

I'm a little thrown. What does he think is going to happen? I'll suddenly decide I need my tits back to make money? Is he concerned about whether I'll regret it? I know they have to make sure you're serious and have thought it through but this seems like a trap, I just can't figure out how.

I ask how much time off I'd need from the business to recover, hoping that's what he means, since I said it was just me running it. That's not what he means.

"If you're selling your body, isn't it prudent to keep everything intact? Surely you'd lose customers if you had this surgery." He sounds like a client giving unsolicited advice on how to do business.

I shake my head. I've done the research and yes, all signs point towards my client base conveniently forgetting/ignoring my trans status. I may essentially be cis for pay, but since I keep being blocked from accessing the transition I want, I see it as simply doing the best I can with the hand I was dealt. I am anticipating losing a lot of clients, sure, but I don't want this guy to be right and I certainly don't want him to offer me business advice.

"Well, kind of, but the more unusual I am, the more niche I become and the more I can charge." I have done the research on this too. "Not to mention I'll be showing up to work more when I'm not dysphoric."

Eventually, he accepts my answers and issues the referral.

I am now 8 months post top surgery and my depression is almost entirely cured. I conduct business with a spring in my step, excited that so many people consider me to be hot in a form I can breathe in. I still think he wanted to deny me again, to make me suffer longer in that body that didn't fit. I can't believe that I had to make a case for the profitability of my body, and that it was accepted over all the times I made the case that it was my body and I should be able to customise it as I see fit.

Submission 12, by A

A Letter to My Girlfriend

A is a trans rent boy with experience in escorting from before transition as well as after, who cannot talk about being a trans hooker without crediting this partner for keeping him afloat.

I wish I could tell the whole world how much you've supported me. The best I can do is to share it anonymously, here, because we live in a place where admitting the ways you've saved me over and over again would put you at risk of arrest. I hate that I can't share how wonderful you are in a way that names you, for fear of how you might be punished. I'll do my best to make my love, and my actions to demonstrate it, enough to make up for it.

When we met, we were both very early in transition. I know you didn't feel it at the time, but I thought you were so beautiful. Whenever people joke about the youthful fashion that a lot of trans people start out with, I remember you in your polka dot skater dresses and me in my button-ups with colourful prints. Both of us were in our late 20s then, and our styles matched. We matched in a lot of other ways, too.

I must have sensed that you wouldn't be judgemental, because you've always given off this welcoming vibe. I told you that I'd been selling sex for a long time and didn't know of any other way to live, which made me too scared to start T when I knew it would lose me clients. I was barely scraping by as it was. I couldn't see a way out and I wanted to die. You told me that you sold sex too, though you'd started only after beginning to transition, and insisted that I would find a way to transition and survive. You told me it wasn't really living if I couldn't be myself and you gave me permission to take the risk.

The thing is, I really did lose clients from transitioning. A lot of my clients had always been racist pricks, who wanted to put a brown woman in her place, and apparently the same appeal just wasn't there when I looked more like my uncle than my mother. The racist abuse got worse as I got more masculine looking, every insult I had ever heard being amplified through the phone I used for escorting, and you were there reassuring me every step of the way. I came out as trans to my clients and started advertising as a man and you told me that I wouldn't go hungry no matter what happened.

We got closer as I rapidly used up the last of the cash I had stored away. I slept at your place any night when I didn't have a client that day or the next – that became most nights. My body began to feel like it was mine and you started to believe me when I told you how pretty you were. I needed to move and had no idea how I'd pay rent anywhere, with paying a deposit sounding like a sick joke, and you told me I'd be staying with you like it was obvious.

I told you how grateful I was at the time, I know. I just don't think I've ever connected the dots for you, that encouraging me to start T and following through on making sure I could still afford to survive kept me from killing myself. It is not over-dramatic to say I would be dead if we hadn't met at our mutual friend's terrible party. Thanks to him too, for bringing us together.

You gained more clients as I lost mine and you covered our bills as I searched for other kinds of work with a huge gap in my CV that I couldn't explain. I'd do gig work and run out of that money so fast that I couldn't afford to travel to see a client when I did get one, so you'd pay for my taxis. I'd get frustrated when a client only seemed to want to sext and not book me and you'd message him for me until he agreed on a time and place. On days where we both had clients to see at home, you'd write down the times that yours were coming so I could easily arrange mine around them (and rearrange yours if they clashed, never mine).

I have no idea how you have such a well of compassion that you were able to commiserate with me about my lack of clients when you were tired from dealing with them all day.

I'd do your make-up when you were going to see a client and try not to mess it up with my kisses after. The men who booked you were more degrading towards you than mine and made so many gross comments that gave you dysphoria. I'd remind you that they were twats whose opinions didn't matter, every time I could. The few clients I would get were calling me "good boy" and yours were acting like your transition was a fetish or pushing for types of sex I know you hate because they liked to make you uncomfortable. You dealt with more of them to make up the difference between my living costs and my earnings. Me being worth that to you still shocks me.

About a year after I found a job outside of sex work, I read up on the law and realized how many times you broke it for me. There were brothel-keeping laws that applied to our flat and laws against you helping me to arrange clients or paying for my transportation to see them. I was always the disorganized one, so you'd help manage things and I never returned the favour. You did that so I could afford things I wanted for myself, back when you were paying all our rent, and I didn't know the risks you were taking for me. Do you remember that you laughed when I came to you, shocked and babbling about all these messed up laws and things you could have been prosecuted for? You apologized after, saying you thought I knew what the laws were and didn't want to make fun of me for only just finding out. I just couldn't get over the idea that you were selling more sex because of me, something I felt so guilty about, and the law would treat you as an exploiter.

It is so unfair that I have to worry about who I admit these things to.

People see us now and learn that you're unemployed, taking a much-deserved break from sex work and happier than I've ever seen you, and they act like I'm such a good guy for financially supporting you. I'd do it no matter what our life used to be like, to see you this happy, but it still feels wrong to say that without acknowledging everything you did. I should be able to tell people about the time you covered our rent and bills and helped me to see clients whenever I could, without worrying they'll label you as a brothel manager and get you into trouble with the police.

I can't name you, but I need people to know how much you've done for me. Almost a decade together now and that makes ten years of life I don't think I'd have had without you.

I love you,
A

Submission 13, by Jack Parker

Paying for Top Surgery, One Dick At a Time

Jack Parker is a British sex worker who has engaged in various kinds of sex work over the last 8 years, from brothel work to online adult content creation to independent escorting. They frequently write about sex work, transness, and the intersection of the two.

Find their work at jackviolet.com.
@mxjackparker across all social media.

I cannot discuss my medical transition without mentioning being a hooker. At every stage, selling sex has been integral to my ability to access transition care. The story of how I managed to get top surgery so quickly after accepting that I'm trans is one that would be completely implausible if I substituted in a different kind of job as my income.

To discuss my transition without mentioning selling sex, I'd have lie so many times by omission and misrepresentation that I might as well make up a whole alternate story.

Here, I'll share the whole truth:

I was already selling sex and making porn when I accepted that I am trans. For years, I had been denying it, forcing myself to act and dress more and more femininely in the hopes that I could suppress it. My sex work persona was a girl-next-door type that I grew out my hair and painted my nails and wore make-up to maintain, appealing to my clients' interests. Under the weight of all that rigidity to my presentation, my egg cracked at almost the precise moment the Covid-19 lockdown began. The sudden break in seeing clients, allowing me to have some breathing room to dress and act the way I wanted, ended the identity crisis I'd been having for years.

Once I admitted that I wanted to transition, suddenly my dysphoria became much harder to tolerate. I'd been dissociating through a lot of my life, refusing to think about my body, and the realization that I could actually do something to change things instead of ignoring them made it feel urgent to transition. The veil lifted and my dysphoria went from a background ache to a stabbing sensation. If I had allowed myself to feel the full weight of it before, feeling like I had no solution, I think it would have killed me.

Since I was barely keeping my head above water financially, I had to push myself harder to save money towards an appointment with a psychiatrist who could give me a gender dysphoria diagnosis. I worked during the Covid-19 lockdown, in spite of the risks and illegality.

My appointment with Dr. Lorimer cost me £360, which I had sex with 3 clients to pay for. Then I needed to pay to see an endocrinologist too, before I could obtain a prescription for testosterone, and I had to suck a couple more dicks to pay for that. Everything I bought, I thought of in terms of the number of clients I had to fuck to make it happen.

If I had access to free and quick transition care through the NHS, there are so many clients I never would have seen. Hours cringing or scowling through thrusts that I wouldn't have experienced. It's amusing to think that the TERFs who wanted to shut down the gender identity clinics entirely are the same SWERFs saying that anything which increases the level of prostitution is evil. Each attack on trans health services contributes to another generation of trans people having to count the cost of their transition in sex acts.

Due to the long wait until my endocrinologist appointment, I decided to buy testosterone online and self-medicate while I waited. Slowly, I changed my work persona into a more androgynous non-binary character followed by rebranding myself as a trans man. I worked a few brothel shifts under the guise of being a cis woman, until it became too risky by 3 months on testosterone, to squeeze out the last of the money I could from my female sex worker persona. By the time I met with my endocrinologist, I was 6 months on testosterone and I had some savings to put towards my transition.

My number of clients shrank when I came out as trans, both in terms of escorting and making porn, but I was still able to get by between bartending jobs and sex work. If I had been content with my medical transition after starting HRT, I could have saved money and been financially stable for the first time in my life. Unfortunately, even though I finally came alive on testosterone and felt like myself, my dysphoria over my chest was overwhelming. I knew I couldn't wait for the best part of a decade to get to a gender clinic through the NHS, to get top surgery. Self-awareness about my

106

desires led to the mounting feeling that I was going to hurt myself or attempt suicide again if I couldn't remove my breasts. Taking off my binder to get naked for clients was almost intolerable.

Much the same as the first time I needed to earn money towards medical transition, I took on more clients as I tried to save towards top surgery. I started a crowdfund to raise some of it, but I knew I wouldn't be able to raise enough before the dysphoria became too much. I worked a full-time bar job and kept selling sex, binding so tight that I had breathing trouble, and I knew I couldn't keep going like that. Paying for the letter which approved me for surgery was easy; affording the surgery itself was not so simple.

I took a lot of risks, earning enough to pay for my double mastectomy. I accepted clients who I ordinarily would have turned down, kept rude clients who treated me poorly as regulars, and I'd answer every call that came through to my work phone. While I faked moaning as if playing a looping track from my mouth, I'd think about how much closer I was getting to my goal of paying for top surgery. A client would grope my breasts until it hurt and I'd dissociate and count backwards from 100 over and over while I thought about how euphoric it would be to have a flat chest. Nothing has ever kept me so motivated to sell sex – I wish I had the same drive back when my look could easily pull in five times as many clients.

No-one at the pub where I bartended knew I was a sex worker, though I told my manager and a few colleagues that I used to work in brothels when I overshared during after-work drinks. The long bar shifts were often worse than seeing bad clients, since at least with clients I only had to tolerate them for an hour or so at a time. I was often targeted for transphobic harassment by the customers at the bar and the physical labour was exhausting. Whenever I thought about walking out and telling my manager to go fuck himself for being so condescending and belittling, I'd remind myself that I needed the money for surgery.

Eventually I hit a wall with my earnings, began to find binding more painful by the day, and I decided to book a consultation with a surgeon. I obtained a date for top surgery that was only a couple of months in the future, with the awareness that I was not getting enough interest from clients to pay for it by then. Dr. Ntanos was professional when assessing my chest and talking me through the results I could expect. He asked me some questions about my goals and I tentatively asked him about the available payment options for surgery. I learned that I could pay half upfront and half after the surgery, so I agreed to a date that was two months in the future despite knowing that I barely had half of the cost of the surgery in my bank account.

Thanks to some luck, the support of my friends, and being paid for a lot of sex, I did manage to get top surgery. Every moment of tolerating clients who irritated or disgusted or bored me was worth it. I would suffer through every violation of my boundaries by clients and every day I was exhausted and sore all over again, if I were forced to do it over. I was so elated with the results that I could hardly believe it was real, and I've never spent money on anything more worthwhile in my entire life.

Of course, after about a week, the bill for the second half of the cost of my surgery came in. I couldn't pay it. I felt immensely guilty, weighing down my relief. Prior to surgery, I was thinking about how I'd rather die than go another day with my breasts attached to me, and suddenly I was free and immensely appreciative to Dr. Ntanos and yet I couldn't show that appreciation by paying the bill.

Selling sex was out of the question for the first couple of months as I healed after surgery, living on the small amount of money I had left and the generosity of friends, so repaying any of this new debt was impossible. I sold bundles of my old porn videos at a discount, telling my fans that they would be the last videos of me with breasts, and barely covered rent. I ignored the e-mails reminding me of the money I owed. Combined with the months I took off from sex work to prepare and then recover, getting top surgery resulted in me losing a huge portion of my client base. I was saddled with this huge debt and my earning potential had shrunk at the same time. Half the chasers who regularly paid me for sex were uninterested as soon as my breasts were gone.

At the time of writing this, over 2 years after receiving top surgery, I still haven't fully paid it off. All the repayments I've managed to make have been paid for entirely by selling sex, which is less lucrative for me now than it was before surgery, and I continue to have frequent financial issues. Admittedly, I see less clients than I theoretically could, but the years of working to my maximum capacity have made me resentful of clients and so damn tired of coddling them through the process of booking me.

Without doing sex work at all stages of transition I could never have afforded HRT or a mastectomy. If not for sex work I'd have been so much more miserable, sleep-walking through life and using substances to numb myself until I reached the end of the gender clinic waiting list, and so I'm glad that sex work was there as an option.

Anyone who wishes I didn't have so many negative experiences whilst selling sex should know that I would have been spared a great number of them if medical transition was free and accessible.

Submission 14, by Anonymous

Anonymous is an avid fan of home STI kits and would like to remind everyone to get tested regularly if they're having any kind of sex.

I show up to the STI clinic knowing that it's going to be an ordeal. Being a trans person already means I get worse medical care, but since I started doing sex work it's gotten so much worse. When the nurse is going through her checklist of questions, she realizes I was last tested for STIs 3 weeks and 4 days ago, and the difficulties begin.

"It's overkill to get tested more than once every 6 weeks," she tells me. I know that recommendation is based on the fact that many STIs take a while to show up in the blood. People tell me HIV can take 6 weeks to seroconvert, as a ballpark figure, all the time.

"Not in my case," I say, hoping she'll continue with the questionnaire.

"How many partners have you had since your last test?" the nurse asks me, smug.

"A couple dozen, I think?"

"Since your last test, not in total."

"Yes, a couple dozen since my last test," I insist.

If I weren't in a rush to get my test done, I might find it a little bit funny to see how scandalized she looks. I'm just annoyed because I know she's going to make this difficult for me and ask me a bunch more questions that I don't need to be asked. She does.

"Okay... that's a high number of sexual partners. Multiple partners puts you at higher risk of..." she jumps into a lecture that includes assumptions that I don't regularly use condoms and that I'm having so much sex because of low self-esteem. Based on the number I gave her, she recommends therapy.

"Sorry, I'm in kind of a hurry and I already know about STI risks. I'm a sex worker. I always use protection. I just need a full range of tests, because I get checked regularly."

The nurse doesn't continue her rant after I interrupt and taps away at her keyboard instead. She's probably logging what I told her, but I didn't give my real GP information so I'm not worried about it ending up on my medical records.

"Alright, we'll get you tested for everything then. We normally don't test people so often, and I see you were last tested less than a month ago, but yours is a special case," she mutters.

Since I told her I sell sex, she hasn't looked me in the eye and has become very focused on her computer screen. I wonder if she's searching up the clinic's policy on treating sex workers.

Her distraction upon learning that I'm a sex worker means she completely skips the rest of the questions she was supposed to ask me. Either she's forgotten that I filled out a form while I was waiting, or she's forgotten what was on it, because she makes another assumption about me and what I need. This one is even more awkward. She collects up some swabs and places them to the side of a tray.

"Right, that's your oral swab and an anal swab, plus we'll do a urine sample. I'm sure you know how to do all those. We'll take your bloods first, then you can do the tests in the bathroom and put all your samples into the box there and head out," she rapidly explains. She's still not looking at me and starts to write notes on the stickers on the collection tubes.

"I need a vaginal swab, too," I tell her.

What was supposed to be a very quick walk-in STI test ends up taking three times as long for me as any of the people I saw go for their appointments before me. I have to listen to yet more lectures from the nurse with information I already know, about birth control and cervical cancer. She recommends me women's services that support sex workers, which are useless to me as someone who is stealth to everyone besides my clients, under the assumption that I'm being abused and want to stop selling sex.

The experience is frustrating and I hate being condescended to. I get what I needed, though. My results are sent to my e-mail and I don't have any STIs.

The next time I call the clinic, a month later, they tell me I got tested with them too recently. I try to explain that I need to be tested more often than average since I'm high risk, but the person on the phone doesn't let me get the words out and tells me it's their policy.

I have to find a new clinic and the process starts all over again.

Chapter 5: Role Models for Transmasculine People

Between the outdated information that doctors parrot and the lies told about HRT by people who are anti-transition, many transmasculine people seek out visuals to get an idea of what testosterone might do to their bodies. Porn featuring transmasculine people who are taking testosterone or have had specific surgeries allows them to confirm the effects with their own eyes. Clinical pictures of bottom growth (clitoral enlargement caused by testosterone) often lack comparisons between the structure when soft and hard and video footage offers far more angles.

The primary intent of the porn we make may be to arouse, but it serves as a record of the effects testosterone on our anatomy and as evidence that we have sexual function. This makes it highly valuable to other transmasculine people, totally separate from whether they might get off to it.

Those who look at porn as research material for their potential future transition aren't necessarily aspiring to be sex workers, however they are still viewing sex workers as a type of role model. We are an example of the changes they can make to their bodies and act as proof that they can still be desirable when they do. Our nudes are probably better quality and frame our t-dicks better too, for easier inspection, than forums and sites where non-professionals post nude transition timelines.

Young trans men sometimes message me with awe at the idea people would pay a transmasculine person for sex and want to know everything I can tell them about the sexualities of my clients. Unsatisfied with noting the views on porn videos with trans men in them, or reading the thirst comments in reply to transmasculine non-binary sex workers' posts, they want to hear about transmasculine people being considered attractive enough to pay for sex with. The invasive questions can get repetitive and frustrating, but they come from a place of anxiety and insecurity that I try to have some respect for; what they're really asking is whether it's possible for us to be considered hot and to be viewed as men at the same time, from someone they think has a larger data set. They soak up our stories about finding clients on Grindr as a way to bolster their self-esteem by proxy.

The nature of our work gives us valuable insight to be shared with other transmasculine people, yet being a mentor to our peers who are early in transition is seen as suspicious. Once we go as far as to share information about how to get started in sex work, for those who seek it, we can face accusations that we are grooming other trans people. We have to be resilient in the face of such complaints from bigots who detest sex workers and trans people, because members of our community continue to need advice on how to stay safe. By the time someone is asking about how to enter into sex work, they've often already decided that they will do it, and the more robust resources which can be found for cis women do not exist for their trans counterparts. Sourcing information directly from trans sex workers is often the only option for people considering the profession to learn.

The few resources that make an effort to be inclusive of transmasculine people will usually include us as an afterthought and only minimal amounts of the advice will apply. Different websites work better for us than for sex workers of other genders, some cam sites have anti-trans policies, and a nervous non-binary person is never going to know if they can get away with working at a specific brothel months into being on testosterone without a trans person who has worked there to tell them!

I asked a few sex workers what advice they found valuable from other transmasculine sex workers, when they first began, and what research they did prior to starting sex work. One self-described 'baby sex worker', who started escorting only a few months before our interview at the age of 18, said, "With no plans for medical transition, I figured my girl friends who do [sex work] would have all the info I'd need. It took me a while to realize that I still needed advice for how to cope with all these clients seeing me as a girl and how uncomfortable it was to edit videos where I was dressed up so femme, and that all came from non-binary people like me or trans dudes thinking about what they did pre-transition." They expressed that they were unsure they would have been able to keep working without the coping methods suggested to them, which included "thinking of it as drag" and "butching it up when you can get away with it."

Direct advice has been vital to many, and others have benefited just from seeing certain services advertised in the first place. I asked a trans man who began sex work in his early forties what made him decide to get into professional domination, so he told me, "I've always had a dominant personality and I like to top. Had no idea people might pay a trans guy for that until I saw a pro-Dom offering his services and thought… that could be me. Hopefully I get to inspire someone else and pass it on, now that I've established myself." Trailblazers are common in the trans community, but we shouldn't need new ones every generation to champion sex work as an option that is possible and is not shameful.

Contrasting the transmasculine people who are fascinated by sex workers who are like them or who are considering beginning sex work for themselves, there are those who think we are making trans people look bad or who have unfair expectations of us. We are resented for the times we cater to the cis male gaze, as if the reason we do so isn't that they're most often the ones opening their wallets. Telling transmasculine people to be authentic or to step outside of the accepted porn archetypes whilst engaging in sex work is advice that many of us cannot take until there is a big shift in the sex industry, because our first priority is always going to be earning enough to survive. Rather than recognizing that sex work is criticized because it is a tool trans people can use to survive, some trans people buy into the idea that the supposed immorality of other trans people is the root of the transphobia against us. Mixing in the feeling many transmasculine people have that selling sex would be an affront to their masculinity, we have the perfect recipe for them to view transmasculine sex workers as a model for what not to do.

Even as we struggle to market ourselves and do sex work in the way that works best for us, we are also expected to be advocates for trans people as a whole. Feeling a need to use their platform to spread educational and progressive content about trans men and transmasculine non-binary people, an interviewee explained, "Any time I worry that being political might be scaring off clients, I remember that the only trans male sex worker a lot of people have heard of is *Buck Angel*, and that someone needs to be out here showing we aren't all transmeds who cozy up to conservatives. Transmascs getting into porn can't be allowed to see him as the blueprint." There is a trade-off to this decision, since a lot of viewers want to avoid a side of politics with their porn, and trans identity is a controversial topic. Posting advocacy content from the same account where we share naked images of ourselves can make us very vulnerable to attack, and this can hit our income.

It can also be hard to overcome the sense that we're not fit to be an example to other trans people, as sex workers. If we enjoy our work with minimal dysphoria and use it mostly as an outlet for our sexual interests, we worry that our relative privilege means we have no right to discuss our jobs and fear glamourizing them. If we hate the work but view it as our best option, engaging in it for our survival, then it can be bittersweet to suggest harm reduction methods to trans people who are in the same position we were in.

I have done my best to make peace with the fact that some transmasculine people will find my content and look up to me no matter what I do, and I'd rather speak honestly about my struggles and my triumphs than have them project onto me. There are still so many sessions of advice-giving and support that I have to pay forward, to make up for all of those which were provided to me with no expectation of repayment.

A few of the people I look up to most in the world are transmasculine sex workers like myself, muddling through and somehow managing to thrive.

Submission 15, by Mister Saul

A Practice of Power and Care

*Mister Saul / Jackson King is a BDSM
practitioner, cultural troublemaker, writer, and
journalist. With appearances across the BBC,
The Guardian, The iPaper and more. He's also
the founding editor of Irresistible Damage
(a magazine for queer trans men) and author of
TESTOSTEROTICA (a trans erotica newsletter).*

Domination has always come from somewhere deep within me. It's a channelling, or hyperfocus. A space I drop down into that's intuitive, instinctive, closely attuned to my submissive, and cruel to be kind.

There are many ways to be a Dominant. You can be mechanical and measured, gleefully sadistic, tender and fatherly, a disciplinarian, an object of worship... and as someone offering paid-for domination services, people approach me with their own definitions and expectations of what a Dominant is. Sometimes we're aligned. Sometimes we're not.

For some, hiring a professional Dominant is a cold, ephemeral exchange. It's a purchase. It's a product: add Spanking Session to cart, then click through to checkout. They get their needs met, the Dominant gets some cash, bish bash bosh and off you go. And all of that is totally fine, in fact more than fine – it's good. But it doesn't speak to me or to my practice of BDSM.

When someone comes to me demanding I be available on short notice, or asking for riskier elements of BDSM without wanting to put the time into careful scene negotiation, I turn them away. Primarily because of safety and wellbeing concerns, but also because it tells me that we aren't working towards the same goal.

I don't really do this for the money (although it's a big plus that covers venue hire costs and compensates me for my time and the resources that go into making a session happen). I do this because I believe in the power of BDSM.

I'm a devotee at the altar of psychically intense embodied experiences and sexual catharsis. If the dungeon is a temple, I am a servant to the space – as well as that interior space opened up by the vulnerability of fetish, fantasy and forbidden desire. I feel in service to something bigger than myself. And this is a service I love offering to my communities, whether Black, trans, queer, or simply a fellow pervert.

I'm conscious of speaking with too much metaphor here. Forgive me. Mine is a developing practice and an area of continued learning and curiosity that I'm still trying to find the right language for. But I imagine many of you reading this will know from personal experience what I'm trying to get at: that consuming and visceral energy that unfolds within a scene. That explicit, intentional and considered embrace of power dynamics alongside erotic self-excavation and exploration of the other in BDSM, which makes it so enticing.

I suspect its raw erotic power is why conservatives and reactionaries work so hard to repress or legislate BDSM away, as well as other sexual cultures of liberated consenting adults coming together for pleasure's (or profit's) sake. While it's true that plumbing the depths of our desires can be heady, sometimes dangerous work, there are many things that are dangerous in our world: hope and love, for example, come with great risk while also promising great reward. I think the risk/reward of BDSM is that you might, in your most vulnerable moment, discover that you are also safe here. Held. By yourself, or someone else.

Power is a really interesting word. I think in our present time it has come to be synonymous with oppression, harm, or abuse. Our lives are so impeded and encumbered by the powers that be and structural powers of oppression. We're subject to politicians drunk with power, or exploitative capitalists for whom money is power. But even the common understanding that power is inherently bad is tempered by the more positive connotations of people power, empowerment and our need for staying power in a system designed to exhaust or even destroy us.

Power can be destructive; it can also be a source of strength and the answer to our greatest challenges as a society. It's this dialectic understanding of power within BDSM that makes it at once so threatening and alluring.

I think each of us has some measure of power, even if drastically limited by forces beyond our control. It can be as impressive as the power to resist and organise, or as subtle as stepping into our own personal power by taking responsibility for what we can.

It's also interesting to me that generally, people feel more comfortable talking about their masochistic rather than their sadistic desires. That it is socially more acceptable to be a submissive than a Dominant: to want to give your power away, than to stand in it. And I get it. I think it's healthy to be cautious of anyone too hungry for power – and to interrogate what such power means to them.

For me, power must be accompanied by care. In fact, I practise domination as a kind of caring: caring enough to spend time learning someone's emotional, sexual and physical needs; caring enough to bring a bespoke fantasy or scene to life, without judgement; and caring enough to embody a power and dominance that a client can safely submit to and find some fulfilment in.

But what does that practice of power and care mean for me personally?

As a Black man, a queer man, and a trans man in Britain, I'm not accustomed to enjoying power. It's a novelty for me that feels exhilarating (while always tempered by care and commitment to the needs of my client). It is a way for me to embrace a personal erotic power that brings pleasure and not harm (although some pain may be involved!) To me, this is an embodiment of power at its best – power exercised in service to something or someone else, while also being an affirmation of the self.

This takes us back to my earlier comment, that being a Dominant is a work of devotion and service. We often think of devotion as the domain of the submissive, but I am devoted to this craft as a Dominant, as well as to the transformative possibilities it opens up for human experience (even if it's as simple as transmuting physical pain into ecstasy).

I suppose what I've spent my wordcount getting at, but not quite naming, is that my practice comes with a sense of deep spirituality. If, by spirituality, we mean the notion that there might be something greater than myself at work when a submissive finds rapture, release, or deep satisfaction down in the dungeon with Mister Saul.

Submission 16, by Ron Beastly

POV: Your Trans Dad Will Always Be Here For You

Ron (he/they) is a 39 year old trans man escort and porn performer/creator based in Bristol, UK. He has copious body hair and a beard envied by many, and loves kink, squirting and good boys/girls/others. He's also an art historian and drag performer, and his life goal is to set up a queer community arts space in Bristol.

Twitter: @RonBeastlyXXX
Website: www.ronbeastly.com

I first started escorting back in 2014, but the amount of admin involved (plus undiagnosed ADHD) led me to take down my adverts after just a few years. I ventured back into the industry in early 2023, making porn alongside escorting. As someone considered too "niche" for most production companies, I was grateful for how much easier it has become to make and distribute porn by yourself. Trans masc porn had evolved since the days of *Bonus Hole Boys*; the variety of amazingly sexy and cool performers was exciting and inspiring, but I wasn't sure where I could fit. At 38 I was significantly older and more bearish than most. I figured I'd just shoot what I liked and keep doing whatever got a response.

For some reason I was surprised when people immediately started calling me "Daddy", and I wasn't sure if I liked it. Testosterone turned me into the spitting image of my own father, who I didn't have a great relationship with and passed away suddenly when I was 22. When I got a request for a video calling myself Daddy, I found editing it strange and not particularly sexy.

Over time, I built a persona I felt comfortable in while harnessing my natural Dad vibes by introducing elements at my own pace and following what my audience responded to. People really liked a picture I posted wearing my reading glasses (I'd just forgotten to take them off) so they became a regular inclusion. I started filming in clothes I kept in the back of my wardrobe for office day jobs and rare formal events. Apparently, looking like a sensible business man while being a total filth pot is a turn on for lots of people, though my vibe is more Geography teacher than CEO. They weren't my day to day clothes, but it never felt like a costume. I wasn't very confident doing role play, so zoom calls became a perfect video premise. They were popular too; one titled POV: You accidentally answer a video call from your Trans Dad while jacking off but it turns out he's into it quickly became my most viewed video.

Being a typical Dom never appealed to me. Saying fun things are punishments seems strange and I'm entirely unable to act stern or pretend I'm not enjoying myself. The "Daddy" persona comes more naturally. I can be warm and goofy, correcting when needed but always with your best interests at heart. I can tell you what a good boy/girl you are and how proud I am. It can tap into the longing many of us have to hear praise from our own fathers, particularly when they've been unable to accept us.

I hope my Trans Dad status grows into more than just a persona I use to sell porn. While 39 isn't particularly old, I came out 24 years ago, much longer than most trans mascs I meet today. I hope he (and I) can give much needed visibility to older trans men and give younger trans guys love, encouragement and the opportunity to imagine the middle aged men they deserve to become.

I love having an outlet to embrace the inevitability of ageing as I approach my 40s, and being an example to those who may not have considered getting older an option.

Submission 17, by Dakota Nevaeh

Dakota Nevaeh is an adult content creator, author, activist, drag/burlesque King, and one of the top Black trans male models on Pornhub.

Twitter: daddypuppy101
Instagram: daddy.puppy101

As a black, gay, trans man, growing up closeted was an incredibly harrowing, yet nonetheless exciting, journey for me. I faced a lot of discrimination and bullying from a young age, both within the community I was forced into and outside of it.

Despite all the hardships, I'm trying my best to stay strong and advocate for LGBTQ+ rights, using my poetry, singing, public speaking, drag, burlesque, modeling, and oddly enough, even sex work! I'm hoping to represent and normalize transgender people in today's society and make the world a better place for others like me.

My goal is never to glamorize sex work. It is dangerous, especially for individuals like myself, and it is very misunderstood. As Americans, I feel we are so closed off from our desires that we allow ourselves to be miserable because of it. I truly believe that if sex work was less taboo and more normalized, there would be less violence.

People often fear what they don't know. That's why I've taken the time, since coming out at age 23, to pop out of my Mormon bubble and experience the world. I feel like I had an extremely slow start to learning about racism and the fact that I was discriminated against and it wasn't my fault. Ever since I found my voice and somebody had the audacity to hand me a microphone at the first protest I went to after George Floyd died, I haven't shut up. I help organize and host "SlutWalk" around the Midwest, a gathering of sex workers and supporters alike all empowering each other. We fight against violence in the sex industry and rape culture, calling for action and calling out abusers. We look out for each other while honoring those who have been murdered.

My personal experiences with sex work, especially trying to do it safely online, have proven to be difficult. I watched a documentary on how a black woman coding a robot which used facial recognition had to use a plain white mask over her face for it to recognize her. To use some online platforms which allow sex workers, facial recognition is required. I was randomly de-platformed, after building a following on one of these sites, and all my videos were deleted. Three years of work deleted with no explanation. I tried re-registering and my face was not recognized, even though I had turned in my ID and scanned my face before. It was crushing, but you get used to being banned and blocked and de-platformed. One cis white male can decide to delete your entire career at the push of a button, meanwhile they program computers to be racist and transphobic.

I am currently one of the top 3 most popular and most viewed black trans male models on Pornhub. I have been for a few years now. I've been doing sex work for 3 years on and off I still feel like my work is in its infancy, and I haven't made more than one thousand dollars. Pornhub actually pays you only 1% of your ad revenue, and sometimes not all of what you put out can be monetized.

Sex workers like me struggle because trans and black people are suppressed and not recognized or respected in the sex industry. There are less opportunities. The fetishization of trans individuals is not something to sleep on, either. There are constant comments like "If you wanna be a black male pornstar you should have a BBC" and "I will destroy that pussy and get you pregnant so you know how to be a real woman!" Being a transmasculine sex worker isn't for the faint of heart.

During my time in sex work, I have to say that almost all of my clients have been cis men. Doing this work has made me fear them, almost not wanting to be like them, which can fuel my dysphoria. It makes it hard for me to talk to women because I don't wanna come off like them. I often end up sounding like a best friend to people who really are interested in my work, instead of being a sexy content seller. To market to cis male clients, you have to put yourself in a box to be seen. I'm currently trying to balance using certain labels to be visible with the fear that doing so could impact the trans community, when it comes to men thinking that they can fetishize all of the trans community.

I'm not entirely proud of the titles of my videos on regular heteronormative websites and platforms. I stereotype myself in them. Although it's not my first choice, labeling myself has led to more engagement on all of the major platforms.

I shoot porn by myself or with my partner. I think the most freeing part about sex work is you can be your own boss, producer, editor, and director. I truly believe sex work is an art. It is a lot of work, and I do struggle with juggling life and making schedules as someone who is on more than just the rainbow spectrum.

I'm currently searching for a trans inclusive and safe production company, to be able to help guide me a bit and show me the ropes in how all this functions for them. My end goal is to exist and to show love people have never seen or thought of before and represent black transmasc sex workers.

Unfortunately, what we call survival sex is also something I've considered, but I fear the danger in meeting strangers that are not also sex workers. It's hard to tell if the fears I have are realistic, or if I'm paranoid, but I think a simple look at statistics justifies my fears as a trans POC. I would like to change that for others and myself. We have a right to safety and security, but being safe and secure is a privilege of cisgender people. As much as I feel responsibility as a protector, I also am coming to terms with the fact that I do not have the power to constantly protect everyone from the dangers of being transgender in America.

The betrayal is never ending from the privileged, that's how they stay privileged. All in all I want to see us thrive; I want to see more from people like me. I want to see trans joy represented, with hope instead of tragedy. I selfishly want to live and see people like me continue to breathe and continue to have resources to be themselves. I wish I had a happily ever after ending to give to everyone reading, but my story has just begun and I thoroughly thank everyone for taking the opportunity to peek into my journey. I am thrilled to be able to do sex work in a safe environment and it has been rewarding regardless of the struggles I've mentioned. I've gained so much self-worth and knowledge breaking bearers and pushing myself into new territories that I never fathomed were possible for me. I want everyone to be able to experience and express themselves in their own personal and beautiful way. Everyone deserves to feel loved and protected and I hope in telling my story so far I can help with that.

Chapter 6: Outside Views: Radical Feminists, Progressives, and the Right

Everyone seems to have opinion on sex work and trans people no matter how uninformed they are. The two topics twined together create complex webs of bigotry in the minds of people committed to certain ideologies.

In the conversation about gender and sex work, a few political groups show up often to give their opinions, repeating their well-known positions: radical feminists view sex workers as prostituted women and victims of sexual exploitation; progressives speak about happy hookers and girlbosses being empowered by selling porn; and conservatives rave about women being sexually immoral by selling sex. Naturally, there are members of any political ideology who break away from the group, but these are some of the common beliefs they espouse. All of these groups tend towards the presumption that all sex workers are women (progressives often including trans women and the others speaking only about cis women). When they are forced to reckon with the existence of men and non-binary people who do sex work, cracks are exposed in their beliefs, leading to some interesting arguments.

It is often not worth directly arguing with whorephobic ideologues themselves. Doing so only exposes you to their audience for harassment. However, it can be helpful to know what to expect when engaging with these different groups online or in public spaces, and understanding the rhetoric allows you to know how to approach the people who listen to those ideologues. Their audiences can be made to understand the reality of gendered experiences within sex work, if we unpack and dissect the faulty assumptions being made.

Sex Worker Exclusionary Radical Feminists (SWERFs)

In simple terms, SWERFs view the sale of sex as paid rape and see porn as filmed sexual exploitation. They argue that payment is a form of sexual coercion which negates consent. These arguments are not inherently gendered, yet SWERFs generally only apply them to women. As they see it, men use money as a means to extract sex from women who have no alternative but to comply, and sometimes they record the abuse to be watched by other men who sadistically get off to it. To them, sex work is a patriarchal invention that allows men an additional way to get access to women's bodies – any woman who claims to choose to sell sex must be mistaken, lacking in self-worth because of sexist ideas she has absorbed or deluding herself as a way to cope with the trauma of engaging in sex work.

Reality is more complex than what radical feminists imagine to justify their disgust reaction towards sex workers. Whilst sex work exists within a patriarchal context, they are wrong that it exists solely for the benefit of male clients over the marginalized. For many of us, sex work is a response to patriarchal oppression, allowing people of marginalized genders and sexualities to profit from the ways we are fetishized and to survive when we otherwise would not. Entitled cisgender heterosexual men did not invent sex work to give themselves an additional way to sexually oppress cisgender women; their entitlement includes the expectation that they should not have to pay. Efforts to criminalize sex work, championed chiefly by men and enforced by groups they populate in large numbers like the police and the courts, demonstrate this well. Misogynistic men do not want women to be able to gain any level of financial freedom, including as a result of sex they may begrudgingly pay for, and so even when they are clients they try to put an end to sex work. Further oppressing people of other marginalized sexualities and genders is sometimes a bonus to them, and on other occasions serves as a primary motivation. If misogynists and bigots wanted us to sell sex, victimizing us in the process, they wouldn't try so hard to legislate against it.

Activists for sex workers rights exist in stark contrast to the victim concept SWERFs believe we embody. Women who sell sex and point out that criminalizing clients would put them in more danger are accused of being members of the 'pimp lobby', but this is not their most effective debate tactic. Members of the general public usually react with disgust or sympathy to women who talk about engaging in prostitution – these are not particularly useful responses, but they don't make someone prone to viewing them as exploiters. The stereotypical pimp, burned into the public consciousness, is a man. This makes men involved in sex work, and trans people who radical feminists can claim are men or are aligned with the interests of men due to our desire to transition, into much better targets for the accusation.

When confronted with the existence of transmasculine sex workers, some SWERFs opt for the argument that transition and sex work are both forms of self-harm undertaken as a result of internalized misogyny. They insist that our clients must view us as women, something they claim we can never stop being, and paint over the reality of our lives with a wash of pink. We are walking contradictions, supposedly transitioning to escape sexism and then seeking out paid misogynistic abuse at the same time.

In cases where a transmasculine sex worker passes as a cis man and claims to enjoy their job, SWERFs sometimes take a different approach. Instead of confused and victimized women who don't know what's best for them, these transmasculine sex workers are framed as gender traitors. The idea behind this phrase is that we are doing things which harm the gender we were assigned as a whole, like encouraging the objectification of women by normalizing sex work. Tactically, SWERFs will sometimes admit that not all sex work is sexual abuse, so that they can argue there is a subset of marginalized people who encourage the existence of the sex trade for our own benefit. They use this idea against transmasculine sex workers by implying that we ultimately seek the role of a pimp or male sexual exploiter, enjoying selling sexual services in the meantime because of our sexual deviancy as we work towards that goal. We are assumed to desire to encourage the degradation of women, only to escape that abuse for ourselves by disguising ourselves among men.

Under the banner of advocating for women's rights, radical feminists seek to infantilize and misgender transmasculine people and treat us as predators when they fail to shove us into their victim category.

The Right

Outside of using sex trafficking scandals and claims that most porn is violent to the point of constituting sexual assault to garner support for bills which harm sex workers, the right do not seek to frame sex workers as sympathetic characters who are suffering. There is a reason that right-wingers are likely to push narratives about middle class women being kidnapped and forced to sell sex whenever they want to use protecting women as an angle to gain support; they view anyone who sells sex by choice (even when heavily influenced by poverty or pressure) as a degenerate. Child safety is one of their favourite excuses to hate us, with their moral panic about minors accessing online porn, and we are blamed for issues which are the result of conservatives' own policies which fail to provide the youth with quality sex education.

High numbers of trans people selling sex, to conservatives, is evidence that we are perverted. Their hatred for trans woman and anyone they can suggest may be one, in addition to their lack of rhetorical use for transmasculine people, means we are ignored in most of their discussions about trans people and sex work. If transmasculine sex workers are mentioned, we are examples of what modern progressive values may lead women and girls towards. We serve as a cautionary tale to teach people who are already primed to hate us that we are the result of a failure to sufficiently control the women in their lives.

Selling sex is not morally wrong, and puritanical ideas about that are easy to dismantle, so the opinion that trans people are especially degenerate because we do it more often can be discarded. Like cis women, we sometimes start because of poverty or because it appeals to us as an enjoyable career or because it is convenient. Excuses about trans people having difficult life circumstances that make us resort to sex work more frequently, often in reaction to conservative policy, should not be the focus of anyone's argument; regardless of how true this is, no-one should need to make an excuse for selling sex when it isn't bad in the first place, and providing these reasons appears like a concession.

One of the few times that transmasculine sex workers are brought up to conservatives is when we are used as a counter to a belief that conservatives hold about their favourite targets, who are trans women. A right wing internet personality will claim that trans women use transition to earn more money in the sex industry than they could as cis gay men, implying that their desire to see as many clients as possible overrides everything else. Responses to this from some well-meaning people include the fact that trans men are restricting their client base by that same logic, yet we also engage in sex work at higher rates, in hopes of exposing the incongruity. However, this inconsistency is of no concern to conservatives, because the reason they give is immaterial. All a right-wing media personality needs to do is point out that a group conservatives already dislike does something their audience considers disgusting, to cement their hatred, and the hypocrisy doesn't matter.

Progressives

Left-wing progressives are much more accepting of sex workers and trans people, on average, than anyone else. Despite this, there are still flaws in how the average progressive who is not well-informed about sex work views our jobs. A lot of the shallow support they show sex workers and the reasons they've accumulated for it rely on simplistic ideas about female empowerment. It is challenging enough for many leftists to maintain their support for sex workers' rights when confronted with those of us who do not enjoy the work, but words often fail them completely when the people they're trying to defend using narratives about women owning their sexuality aren't even women. Broad statements made by them about sex work tend to use the same gendered language that conservatives and radical feminists do, defaulting to "she" and "her" in hypotheticals, and their analysis of whorephobia fails to recognize that it is not exclusively a means of suppressing women's sexuality. Their understanding of the gendered dynamics is limited.

Misunderstandings experienced by leftists can be corrected much more easily than malicious intentions or a strict ideological opposition to our identities. Someone who is otherwise progressive and cares about trans people can be made to understand the complexities of our experiences in sex work and what they say about the gendered nature of the bigotry against sex workers. Unlike staunch conservatives or radical feminists, they may shift their views over the span of a few conversations.

Paid sexual labour is not inherently more liberating than uncompensated sexual activities are, and it is often far more restrictive because it's harder to cater to your own preferences in a sexual partner or cam sex buddy when you're limited to people who are willing to pay. Earning money being paid for sex will feel empowering to some women on the basis that they are breaking one of the ultimate sexual taboos, but for most the only thing that's giving them more influence or resources or fulfilment is the money. A longing to break down misogynistic expectations as a strong woman is not required for an empowerment narrative to fit, and more importantly sex work shouldn't have to be empowering to be considered valid labour. Progressives seem to understand this principle when it comes to other jobs, with many working class leftists commiserating over their struggles in retail jobs or construction or kitchens and fighting for improved workers' rights. Suddenly they have difficulties when the worker in question is a trans man who feels uncomfortable with the ways he is viewed by his clients, but who does sex work to pay his bills.

Obliviousness is also common among progressive groups about how high the demand for sexual services from transmasculine people is. Unlike conservatives or radical feminists, they're likely to have friends who are trans and to be around people who aren't afraid of expressing their attractions to trans people. This means they are likely to have a skewed idea of how many clients or customers we are likely to be able to pull in. They will likely presume parts of our experiences are the same as our peers who are women, because that's what they know the most about, and it can be frustrating to explain the difference in demand between masculine and feminine gender presentations.

Sex workers and trans people are far more likely to be progressives ourselves than the average member of the population, because of the attacks on us from conservatives and radical feminists alike and the demographics within our communities, so the lack of understanding from other leftists can be especially painful. The fact they are close to allyship, yet fall short, is a source of frustration.

The damage done to transmasculine sex workers by whorephobic and anti-transmasculine views is both material and psychological. Propaganda about sex work and transness takes root in the minds of our families and friends, leading them to invalidate our genders because we're sex workers, while support services for sex workers fail to meet our needs because lobbying groups make them unwilling to acknowledge gender diversity in the industry.

Explaining the dire need for an end to transphobia in porn and from clients requires highlighting transmasculine sex workers' experiences of trauma and abuse, and these accounts are used as evidence that our autonomy should be taken from us because sex work is damaging. Focusing on the positive experiences, like examples of us becoming confident in our bodies through charging for access to them, leads to accusations that we are hiding the harms done to sex workers by clients and partners and the police instead.

Though the cost may be high for us individually, the only way to combat the lack of understanding and insistence on ignoring the diversity of our experiences is to share them honestly and come together in numbers. There are trans men who are miserable performing as women at strip clubs a few nights a week, non-binary people with audiences to their online jacking off sessions who are thrilled to have such fun jobs that help them to save for surgery, and transmasculine rent boys who feel completely ambivalent about letting clients have sex with them. Some of us do sex work that feels like cis gay cruising with cash involved and have never felt more masculine, others feel trapped and suffocated by clients expecting us to be feminine. Any opinion that is formed without an understanding of the variety within our community will always be flawed.

Submission 18, by Rush

Little Deals, Not a Big One.

Rush is a jack of all trades. He's a Grindr expert and gig economy slut with a system for seducing his way into some extra cash. He isn't a writer by nature but is willing to commit words to paper if he has something to say and speaking just won't do.

I only started thinking about myself as a sex worker super recently. Feel free to think I'm an idiot for that, 'cause my friends have all been saying it, but it didn't occur to me that guys pay me for sex until I said it out loud to another person: I complain to guys on dating apps about my lack of money while we sext, then act like I'm a bit reluctant to go to their place to fuck, and I go if they connect the dots and offer me money.

Wasn't even trying to hide it from my friends, since I knew they wouldn't give a shit. I'd mention texting some guy from Grindr or tell them I was trying to get money from someone I knew so we could afford alcohol for a party, just didn't fully connect the two. They didn't seem totally connected to me, anyway, as anything more than proof of my amazing multi-tasking skills.

I find guys I want to fuck and I also try and talk those guys into giving me cash. I talk people into giving me little bits of pocket change all the time, 'cause I grew up with no money and it's something I've needed to master. Sleeping around is fun and my friends know me for being kind of a slut, and people have their brains shut off a bit when they want sex so that's the time they're most likely to easily agree to hand over money. I knew I was hustling them but I didn't realize I was, y'know, *hustling*. Sex work seemed like the name for something more formal and intentional than my fucking around.

I've never had a paid hook-up go worse than a free one. More of them have daddy vibes, I guess, and they're usually a little more into me being trans instead of it being an incidental thing. Probably just that the ones who are super into me, and up for paying a bunch of money 'cause of that, are pretty likely to have a thing for dudes with pussies. Doesn't feel like a guy giving me some money changes much, other than him being more eager and able to afford to spare the cash.

Had to hype myself up a bunch to share this, 'cause it feels like such an underwhelming thing to talk about. I always ask for extra dips or fries or an extra piece of chicken when I go out to eat, to see if I can get it for free, and that doesn't feel like some big fucking deal. Asking for money from a guy I'm up for sleeping with, in addition to the sex, feels kinda similar. I've started making a point of talking about being a sex worker, though, after I heard the questions my friends had to ask about it.

Everyone I hang out with, who are all generally super chill, had stuff they wanted to ask about whether I was being safe or what it was like. I've never hidden how much I sleep around from them, or how I meet these guys on hook-up apps and know nothing about them, so the questions were especially nuts. I don't think anyone's more likely to go axe murderer on me when there's a little cash involved. I'm not asking for enough money that anyone's going to fight me over it. Whatever my friends imagine sex work is supposed to be like just overwrites what they know about me and how I live, and it's the fault of stereotypes that have nothing to do with me. Except if people closer to the stereotype are the only ones talking 'cause people like me don't think of ourselves as sex workers, my friends and the friends of other sluts for pay like me are going to keep assuming stuff that's false. I'll do my part to fix it by picking up the monicker.

I'm not a spokesperson and I'm not up for giving my opinions on a load of policy stuff that I don't really understand. I just think it's worth mentioning that guys like me exist, who charge for sex and who it isn't a big deal for.

Submission 19, by Eric

I Don't Like Sex. I Love My Cat.

Eric is an asexual trans man who experiences a degree of sex repulsion. His cat is his incentive to keep doing sex work. Her collars and treats aren't free.

"You're such a slutty girl for me, you love this."

He says this a lot. I'm a man, not a girl. I don't like him. I don't like sex. I nod and pant. I clench and unclench.

"That's it, cum on my dick."

I have never had an orgasm with him. I have never had an orgasm with a client. I don't masturbate when I'm on my own. I don't really get turned on. I don't get attracted to people. I'm asexual.

"Such a pretty pussy."

I hate that word. I don't like to call my parts anything. I call them my parts or say front hole if I have to refer to it.

Silence. He cums. He gets off me. He takes the condom off and throws it in the little bin in my room. He gets dressed. He leaves.

I count my money after he goes. It doesn't feel like a lot any more. The money felt like a lot when I started. It still feels like enough. It's so easy. Any money is good when it's so easy. It doesn't have to be a lot.

The next guy doesn't talk about how much he thinks I like it. I don't really pretend to. I think sometimes they pretend to themselves that I seem like I enjoy it. It's good that they can do the pretending. I am not a very good actor.

"Why do you do this?"

He waits until after he cums to ask me. Maybe he was worried I'd say something really sad. Saying sad stuff kills boners.

"I like money."

It's true. I pick the nicest way to say it.

"Heh. If I looked like you, I'd probably do the same. You get to have great sex and get paid. Seems like a great deal to me!"

He would do it if he looked like me. I think he means girly and pretty. I hate that. I hate him. Why did he say great sex? It feels weird that he liked the sex. I needed to pee the whole time. I still need to pee. It burns a bit because I've had a lot of sex today.

148

He leaves as quick as the last one. I'm done. I take off my wig. I take off my make-up. I pee. I shower. I have to wash my parts thoroughly or I'll feel disgusting later. It's annoying.

I put on my binder after the shower. I wear my comfy clothes on top and it's like my chest is getting a tight hug underneath. It's nice. I go to the mirror and look at myself. I don't look girly or pretty. I look handsome.

I put all my money on my bed and get out the folder my friend made me. I put money in all the compartments for different bills. I have some money left. That money can be used for toys and cute things for my cat. I feel fine having sex I don't like and being called girly by clients if it means I can buy nice things for her.

I'm the cat dad version of a single parent selling sex to feed their kids.

Submission 20, by Sunan

An Interview

Sunan loves hiking and climbing. He does sex work so he can afford to keep doing those activities in his free time, which have been more difficult for him since he was injured but are still his favourite things to do.

For his contribution, Sunan chose some questions he would like to answer in an interview style, transcribed here.

When did you start doing sex work?

I found it really hard to keep a job my whole life. I have autism and I get burned out really easily and I don't know how to do a lot of things. You know how like, people say everyone's good at something? I think all my things I'm good at aren't stuff I could get paid to do as a job, and jobs I did get had bosses that didn't explain things clearly and expected me to do all these things as part of the job without telling me. My family helped a lot with my rent and wanted me to be independent so they didn't have to and I kept trying.

Escorting or making sexy videos was something I knew I could do, and there would be no boss with all these extra rules and I couldn't get fired and I wouldn't have to work almost every day. I though about it a lot, but like, as an idea for if stuff got really bad and I couldn't do another job and my family couldn't help any more.

A couple of years ago I ended up in the hospital with a bad head injury. Lots of things were really hard after and I couldn't work and my family didn't believe me about what happened. I did lots of searching on the internet and found some forums and they explained how to do adverts and I thought I was allowed to do escorting now because I couldn't do other jobs and so it was okay. I don't think people need an excuse like that to do it now but I did before I started.

Does your injury make anything different for you while doing sex work?

I never did escorting before the TBI and I don't know how I would have done without it, but I have, like, asked other escorts if they have the things happen to them that happen to me and they say they don't and I know some of them are from how I act and talk now.

So, I didn't talk about the TBI to my clients because I was embarrassed and it's awkward. One of my new friends who is also an escort told me it's good that I didn't because lots of clients would take advantage and book me because I seem vulnerable and stuff.

I've had a lot of clients tell me they think I'm drunk or high and even the ones who don't say that seem to think that I am. Sometimes I go on review forums, and I know I'm not supposed to do that and it's bad for my mental health but I do, and I see lots of them saying I seemed out of it and that they think I must drink too much. One of them said my make-up is always shaky like I was drunk when I put it on or I slept in it and that made me sad.

You mentioned make-up, so that's a good way to lead into the next question. What gender presentation do you use for work?

I don't say anything about my gender because it would make me really sad to call myself a girl and I hate lying.

I wear make-up and dresses though, and my profile says female because that's what is on my license and I don't tell my clients I'm not. They all think I'm a girl and I know that the way I dress up is playing into that or making them think that more so I guess it is still kind of lying.

The underwear I use for work is also women's stuff instead of like, boxers and stuff that I usually wear. I haven't thought about that before, but yeah, that's not something I like and I only do it for the clients.

Why do you use that kind of presentation?

Getting doctors to listen to me has been really hard and so I haven't been able to, like, get on testosterone or get surgery yet. I know I don't look like a man and everyone will see me as a lady anyway so I don't think it's worth all the effort to tell clients about being trans and then it makes more sense to do make-up and wear dresses because that's what I see everyone else do in their adverts and stuff.

I'm used to doing it now and I think it would feel weird for a while if I didn't. Like, if I told clients a guy's name and said I'm trans and wore my normal clothes I think it would be strange. My dresses are like a work uniform and I have a way I do my make-up for work and I think all that makes it harder to recognize me from my work pictures too. All that stuff is good so I can keep work separate from the rest of my me-time and do things I like and not worry about people finding out too much.

What do you like to do outside of work?

I really love to go on long walks and hikes and do climbing! Climbing is a lot more with trees or structures that I find, instead of climbing walls, but I know climbing walls with the ropes attached are safer and I'm trying to go to those more often since my head injury.

The escorting helps me pay for new hiking boots which my parents would never get for me before when I needed them to pay for stuff. I don't like lots of types of them because they're pinchy and they take a long time to break in and the ones I do like are really expensive.

Any final thoughts you want to share?

I think it's important that people know I'm still an adult and I can make my own choices as a trans person and an escort and have autism and have a TBI at the same time. I know what I'm doing and people shouldn't tell me what I want or what I should do like they know that better than me.

Submission 21, by Trip Richards

The Need For Nuanced Narratives

Trip Richards (aka TripleXTransMan) is a transgender man, sex worker, and educator. After working in almost every adult industry sector over the past 11 years, he currently focuses on content creation. Trip's advocacy work is centered on demystifying the transgender experience, normalizing the transgender body, and improving working conditions for erotic laborers.

I am a transgender man and a sex worker. Within a year of beginning my medical transition back in 2015, I had grown enough facial hair and masculinized my body shape sufficiently that most people assumed I was a cisgender man as long as I kept my clothes on. However, people frequently meet me with my clothes off. During my 11 year career in the adult industry, (I started prior to my transition) I have done a little bit of everything including webcamming, BDSM work, escorting, studio porn, indie porn, content creation, and erotic massage.

I think a lot about the ways in which my career has influenced my own identity as a queer trans man. My lived experience as a sex worker exists in contrast with common narratives that doing sex work is a result of trauma, lack of alternatives, sexual depravity, or that the work also damages us in these specific ways. Instead, my work has directly confronted my pre-existing feelings of disempowerment and internalized bodily shame. It has fostered my sense of power and autonomy, and has been eye opening as I found that my body and work is at the center of sociopolitical debate.

Sex work is concrete and personal. As a young trans man, my gender was affirmed by my gay male clients, and those formative experiences of validation are integral to my current confidence. When I speak about experiences, I don't just mean good sex, although of course that's part of it. I mean learning how to relate to diverse people, and how to offer them kindness and gentleness with the expectation of mutual respect. I mean providing healing, education, and reassurance through my words, and yes, my touch. I mean recognizing the power of my own body, and the importance of pleasure and safety. And I also mean the imperative of self-advocacy.

As a transgender sex worker, I must continually be an activist for my own right to exist. I am continuously told that neither my body nor what I do with my body are acceptable in society. My body is labeled a "disgusting mutilated abomination" (standard transphobic language on the internet) and yet it's also the body that pays all my bills and brings me all my embodied human pleasure. And the people who pay my bills – yes, the often-maligned "johns" and other clients – are overwhelmingly lovely normal human beings whose motives range from desire to curiosity and back again. Even to the extent that I am fetishized, it is largely on my own terms and at a price point that I set myself.

Although I support language like #SexWorkIsWork, I don't believe that erotic labor is quite the same as any other job. Flattening complex phenomena into the singularity of "work" misses the unique complexities. For one thing, sex workers are systematically excluded from positions of policy making, popular media, and public space. The same language that is used to question our choice to do sex work is also used to question our ability to advocate for ourselves. I've been repeatedly told that I'm too biased to speak about my own profession. I am also often told that I am too dumb – specifically a "dumb whore" – to speak about my own experiences. Yet nobody is more of an expert on the complex conditions of sex work than sex workers ourselves. Sex workers are some of the most astute and knowledgeable individuals I've ever met.

When we are excluded from policy, just like when we are excluded from the visible public sphere, we are at the mercy of other people's moralizing and often deeply biased perspectives. Due to social attitudes toward sex, sexuality, and people who offer sexual services, it's challenging for many people to approach us openly and include us meaningfully.

When we are included in a tokenized way, we often feel pressure to conform to easily digested narratives that ignore our complicated and often contradictory labor experiences. Throughout my career, I have walked a tightrope between the simplified poles of "glamorous pornstar" and "marginalized minority." My inconveniently nuanced reality is one that doesn't fit well into sound bites or social media posts. Reality is further complicated by the fact that sex workers are so diverse and have such diverse experiences. Race, gender (actual and perceived), ability status, and geographic location are some of the many factors that impact success including income.

I am a cis-male-passing, able-bodied, white-passing trans man who is a native speaker in the country in which I work and reside. This has conferred incalculable privilege to my experience of sex work. These privileges show up not only in my direct work environments such as customer interactions, but also in my access to opportunities like writing and speaking gigs where I can share my perspective. However, even this significant privilege does not insulate me from harassment, violence, criminalization, financial discrimination, deplatforming, targeted transphobia and homophobia, and economic precarity. Although we cannot say that there is any singular sex work experience, nor that there is any particular kind of person who becomes a sex worker, it's safe to say that all sex workers experience unique hardships created by public policy and opinion.

I often feel unable to speak about these genuinely problematic elements of my work without my words possibly being used against my colleagues and I in ways that would further marginalize us. When sex workers talk about difficult situations we have endured, we are often told simply to "get a [different] job." This silencing is intentional and oppressive.

As laborers, we must all have space to critique our collective material realities under capitalism. Although the language of exploitation is often weaponized against sex workers, it's rarely contextualized through the lens of capitalism, in which all labor is literally a matter of "selling one's body." Furthermore, as erotic laborers, we also need to have space to discuss the unique challenges we face from systemic criminalization and dehumanization that targets us specifically due to our careers. These conditions are not inherent to "work" but rather specific to "sex work," and that's why I see #SexWorkIsWork as a well-intentioned but incomplete sentiment.

Broadly speaking, it's not my work itself that I find difficult, but rather the attitudes I experience from people who are not even part of my work.

The fact that so many sex workers have positive experiences in spite of these negative factors confronts assumptions about our industry. As I approach the end of my own performing career, I feel pride and satisfaction. For me, sex work has been personally and economically transformative. Some of the qualities I like best about myself – my kindness, my capacity to communicate, my belief in my value, my understanding of humanity - were honed through my work. I hardly recognize the person who first took their clothes off on the internet, and not just because of the physical changes from years on testosterone!

Trigger Warnings

Submission 1 – Transphobia, Border Crossing Discrimination.
Submission 2 – X
Submission 3 – Transphobia, Misgendering, Whorephobia, Discussion of Gender Dysphoria, Drug Use Mentions, Alcohol Mentions, Homophobic Slurs.
Submission 4 – Transphobia, Police Mentions.
Submission 5 – Transphobia, Homophobia, Genital Mentions.
Submission 6 – Graphic Sexual Descriptions, Genital Mentions.
Submission 7 – Graphic Sexual Descriptions, Genital Mentions.
Submission 8 – Transphobia, Anti-Asian Racism, Anti-Black Racism, Racial Slurs, Genital Mentions, Homophobic Slurs.
Submission 9 – Transphobia, Sexual Abuse, Domestic Abuse, Verbal Abuse, Mental Health Issues, Discussion of Gender Dysphoria.
Submission 10 – Transphobia, Sexual Abuse, Genitalia Mentions, Discussion of Gender Dysphoria.
Submission 11 – Transphobia, Transmedicalism, Surgery Mentions, Fatphobia, Medical Discrimination, Suicide Mentions, Whorephobia.
Submission 12 – Transphobia, Racism, Suicide Mentions.
Submission 13 – Transphobia, Discussion of Gender Dysphoria, Dissociation Mentions, Surgery Mentions, Suicide Mentions.

Submission 14 – Transphobia, Medical Discrimination, Whorephobia, Genital Mentions.
Submission 15 – Discussion of BDSM.
Submission 16 – X
Submission 17 – Transphobia, Anti-Black Racism, Religion Mentions, Abuse Mentions, Murder Mentions, Genital Mentions.
Submission 18 – Alcohol Mentions, Genital Mentions.
Submission 19 – Transphobia, Misgendering, Graphic Sexual Descriptions, Genital Mentions, Gender Dysphoria Discussion, Sex Repulsion Discussion.
Submission 20 – Transphobia, Brain Injury Mentions, Ableism.
Submission 21 – Transphobia, Whorephobia.

Survey Snapshot of Transmasculine Sex Workers

Here are a small selection of some of the surveys I collected from transmasculine sex workers, in the process of putting together this anthology and considering what topics it should focus on. Some of the respondents were then interviewed, to get more in-depth information about their experiences.

Almost everyone who responded to these surveys answered that doing sex work had impacted their choices about transition, with a large proportion of those who did sex work before *and* after transitioning reporting that they had delayed elements of their transition for the benefit of their work.

112 responses would seem like a small sample size to me, in a lot of contexts, but I admit that the number of answers I've gotten felt huge when I first saw it. I couldn't fathom more than a handful of workers like myself existing when I first considered transitioning while continuing to do sex work, and suddenly with a single post I can connect to over a hundred.

1

What is your gender identity?: Non-binary.

What kinds of sex work have you engaged in?: Webcam modelling.

When have you engaged in sex work?: Both before and after transitioning (socially or medically)

How long have you engaged in sex work? (Or how long did you engage in sex work?): More than 10 years

Who in your life knows that you do sex work?: Only the people who are close to me.

Have you experienced physical violence whilst engaging in sex work?: Yes

Have you experienced mistreatment from clients for being transgender?: No

What are your thoughts on how being a transmasculine person has impacted your experience in sex work?: some clients said or implied that they felt "safer" with me than a cis-male, which was definitely something I had to process in therapy

Has sex work impacted your choices about transition, and how? (Such as whether to get certain surgeries, when you came out, etc.): impacted coming out, staying closeted in certain circles for much longer

2

What is your gender identity?: Trans man.

What kinds of sex work have you engaged in?: Selling or trading sex in-person (full service sex work).

When have you engaged in sex work?: Before transitioning (socially or medically)

How long have you engaged in sex work? (Or how long did you engage in sex work?): 2 – 3 years.

Who in your life knows that you do sex work?: No-one.

Have you experienced physical violence whilst engaging in sex work?: Yes

Have you experienced mistreatment from clients for being transgender?: Yes

What are your thoughts on how being a transmasculine person has impacted your experience in sex work?: I know that there are people in my life who would be less accepting of me being trans if they knew I had done this, so I'm more secretive. I stopped shortly after I came out, because my clients got worse and I was so paranoid about being seen by someone who knew me.

Has sex work impacted your choices about transition, and how? (Such as whether to get certain surgeries, when you came out, etc.): It's opened up options for me that I wouldn't have without it. I'll be getting double incision in 4 months with money I made doing sex work.

3

What is your gender identity?: Bigender.

What kinds of sex work have you engaged in?: Stripping. Webcam modelling. Selling used panties, socks, etc. Creating and selling porn including myself.

When have you engaged in sex work?: Before transitioning (socially or medically)

How long have you engaged in sex work? (Or how long did you engage in sex work?): 2 – 3 years.

Who in your life knows that you do sex work?: Only the people who are close to me.

Have you experienced physical violence whilst engaging in sex work?: No.

Have you experienced mistreatment from clients for being transgender?: No.

What are your thoughts on how being a transmasculine person has impacted your experience in sex work?: Sex work can be pretty wrought at the best of times, with little in the ways of means to protect myself and worries about the repercussions of trying to stay out of poverty. But in my circumstance, while I never faced violence while I worked, the threat was always there that, if any of my clients discovered I was trans, I could face danger. A lot of clients were demanding or insulting, and could have easily done worse if they had thought I 'tricked' them.

Has sex work impacted your choices about transition, and how? (Such as whether to get certain surgeries, when you came out, etc.): Yes.

What is your gender identity?: Trans man. Non-binary.

What kinds of sex work have you engaged in?: Creating and selling porn including myself.

When have you engaged in sex work?: Both before and after transitioning (socially or medically)

How long have you engaged in sex work? (Or how long did you engage in sex work?): 1 – 2 years.

Who in your life knows that you do sex work?: Only the people who are close to me.

Have you experienced physical violence whilst engaging in sex work?: No.

Have you experienced mistreatment from clients for being transgender?: Yes.

What are your thoughts on how being a transmasculine person has impacted your experience in sex work?: There are seemingly only two or three stereotypes you have to make yourself fit into to get any traction – skinny hairless cherubic twink that passes, huge hairy bear that passes, or not passing and doing high-risk/violent kinks (cnc, corrective r*pe, forced feminisation, knife play, etc etc). It was very difficult to actually make any money, and the trauma from how I was expected to market myself to very violent sadists bc I couldn't pass really outweighed the money made. It just wasn't sustainable.

Has sex work impacted your choices about transition, and how? (Such as whether to get certain surgeries, when you came out, etc.): No.

What is your gender identity?: Non-binary. Trans man.

What kinds of sex work have you engaged in?: Selling or trading sex in-person (full service sex work). Creating and selling porn including myself. Webcam modelling. Professional domination.

When have you engaged in sex work?: Both before and after transitioning (socially or medically)

How long have you engaged in sex work? (Or how long did you engage in sex work?): More than 10 years.

Who in your life knows that you do sex work?: Everyone in my life knows.

Have you experienced physical violence whilst engaging in sex work?: No.

Have you experienced mistreatment from clients for being transgender?: No.

What are your thoughts on how being a transmasculine person has impacted your experience in sex work?: Trans masculine people are the least desired in sex work (because we arent fetishized as much) so in order to continue being successful and surviving, I've had to fly under the radar. I am feminine presenting anyway so this is easier for me than many others, but it does impact me. I am sometimes mis-interpreted as being transfem or "secretly" transfem which is awkard to navigate. I have not experienced any violence due to not being out in a professional capacity. I worry about what will happen when my facial hair gets harder to hide (5 o clock shadows, etc) and i have to be very careful about where i participate in online trans masc communities (or even dating apps) out of fear that clients will see me there and realize im not a woman. It has led to isolation.

Has sex work impacted your choices about transition, and how? (Such as whether to get certain surgeries, when you came out, etc.): Yes, I am limited in many ways by my need to present as believably female.

What is your gender identity?: Trans man.

What kinds of sex work have you engaged in?: Creating and selling porn including myself. Paid phone sex. ProDom (online). Findom (online).

When have you engaged in sex work?: Both before and after transitioning (socially or medically)

How long have you engaged in sex work? (Or how long did you engage in sex work?): 2 – 3 years.

Who in your life knows that you do sex work?: Only the people who are close to me.

Have you experienced physical violence whilst engaging in sex work?: No.

Have you experienced mistreatment from clients for being transgender?: Yes.

What are your thoughts on how being a transmasculine person has impacted your experience in sex work?: I came out, and changed basically nothing about my presentation etc, except that I now went by different pronouns, terms of address and gender identity. I think it's affected my sex work in that I'm not 'masculine enough' for one crowd, or I'm 'too feminine' for another and not using female as my gender identity (even tho literally nothing else changed), I've really noticed a difference in my following and earning potential, both dropped by a lot.

Has sex work impacted your choices about transition, and how? (Such as whether to get certain surgeries, when you came out, etc.): I don't want to medically transition at the moment at all, irrespective of my sex work. But for socially transitioning, it's helped me be more assertive about wanting to have my gender/pronouns respected by family etc. I originally did sex work and identified as a woman, but found it so exhausting, difficult and soul destroying, that I came out as trans masc and I think it massively affected my following and earning potential.

Transmasculine Guide to Sex Work, by Jack Parker

(Originally published on the 4th of January 2023 on jackviolet.com)

This is a resource which breaks down how to navigate various types of sex work as a transmasculine person, what kinds of places to advertise, how to stay safe, and the issues you can expect to face as a transmasculine sex worker.

Through publishing it, I have received messages from hundreds of transmasculine people who either already do sex work or intend to do it in the future. They've shared their stories with me and connected me to such a rich community that I could not be more grateful.

Not all of the advice in the article below will work for everyone, and it is all filtered through the bias of my own experiences implementing (or failing to implement) these suggestions.

If you're a trans man or transmasculine non-binary person and a sex worker (or want to be a sex worker) then most resources aren't going to be built with you in mind. The few resources that make an effort to be inclusive will have you as an afterthought and only minimal amounts of advice will apply. I decided to create this as a resource for transmasculine people specifically, without a need to wade through a lot of information that won't help you.

My advice will vary greatly depending on your current personal situation, and so some of the information offered will only be applicable for trans men and transmasculine non-binary people in certain situations and will be labelled to make it skippable. I will speak about both online content creation and selling sex in-person, and I will make it clear which I am speaking about.

If you are not yet medically transitioning, or do not intend to, and either you do not yet do sex work or you currently work under a female alias:

Delay coming out as trans within your sex work persona for as long as possible. If you do not already sell online content, or have not sold escorting services before, you will make far more money doing either if you pretend to be a cis woman. If you do not intend to medically transition, you can do this for as long as you like (unless or until you can no longer tolerate it). Weigh up whether it is worth it for you, in terms of selling sex or porn with a female persona, noting the money you earn versus the severity of dysphoria it may cause you.

For online sex workers in this situation, when coming out: Create content in bulk prior to any medical transition milestones, so that you can keep posting it even when you are further along on T or have had top surgery. Once you do decide to come out as trans to your audience, you should have videos and pictures already filmed that you have not posted, while you were still using those created prior to medically transitioning. Post some of these images in coming out posts across your social media and release a couple of videos at the same time. These videos should ideally be showing off new features since medical transition, like bottom growth if you're on T and experience that, or roleplay videos with a premise about coming out to a partner or having sex early in transition and being affirming. Set the new tone.

For those selling sex in-person: Inform regular clients personally, when you come out. Do not rely on them checking your ads or social media and getting nasty surprises. You can tell them in person or over the phone, or simply cut them off and stop seeing them once you come out if you think they are likely to be unsupportive or angry. If you are unsure, prior to coming out publicly on your escorting ads and profiles you can drop hints that you're thinking about it or ask their opinions. Be prepared that you will lose regulars over this, or that many of those who stick around will only do so for a little while until you transition more and may discourage you against it or still refer to you with very feminine terms. You can decide if it's worth tolerating for you.

Regardless of which sector of sex work you're involved in, it is a good idea to keep a hold of all pre-transition nudes and/or videos that you have. I always recommend that escorts sell porn on the side for some extra income, especially because sites like Adultwork have functionality for you to sell videos on their site and having videos there makes people more likely to book you after watching them if you're trans and they're unsure about how masculine you are just from pictures and want video footage in sexual situations. Either way, keeping older content is a good idea to be used at a later date. Usually, after a total rebrand, we eventually retire old content. You'll remove pre-transition images from your escorting profile or pre-transition videos from your Onlyfans or ManyVids or IWantClips or whatever sites you use. You can then, later, with new clients who never saw you pre-transition, sell these kinds of clips or

173

images at a much higher rate to clients who are chasers or who are curious as to what you looked like "before". You can suggest it's embarrassing for you (some of them are into the idea that you're humiliated by it) and thus you have a high price.

For those who do not yet do sex work and are already medically transitioning, or who already do sex work openly as a transmasculine person whether transitioning medically or not:

Make your ads extremely clear with regards to your identity. Clients often have very little knowledge about trans people, even when they are chasers. Even if you think it is obvious, I promise you, you can stand to be more obvious! Especially given the hypervisibility of trans women in sex work, if you have "trans" in your profile – even if you have "trans *man*" – you may be assumed to be a trans woman regardless of how you look or present.

With online work, I would suggest considering having at least a couple of entirely nude pictures which you make freely available. This clears up any confusion regarding genitals or your chest, whether you've had any kind of surgery or not. Particularly regarding bottom growth, there will be a lot of clients who want to see it and many who are curious but attached to a "straight" identity who want to see your genitals before they'll be willing to subscribe to a site like Onlyfans or directly buy your videos.

To make escorting ads clear, you want to have multiple levels of explanation for people at various levels of familiarity. For example, consider putting "FTM" in your username (even if you're non-binary, if you're on T or have top surgery). Your tag line on an escorting site, as well as your bio, should contain phrases like "FTM trans man with a pussy" or "FTM trans man with B-cup tits" etc. Name body parts you have or that have been altered by surgery. If you're comfortable taking off your binder and/or with clients touching your chest, list cup size so it's clear you haven't had top surgery. Ideally, have pictures of yourself wearing a binder and also not wearing one if you wear one generally, and include a private gallery of nudes (which you can charge for on many escorting sites).

For any transmasculine person, regardless of whether they're already doing sex work, who intends to do sex work:

It is vital that you work out where to advertise what, and that you don't rely on where cis people have their success. Ask other transmasculine people where they have success in advertising, even if it is in completely different places. Advertise on a wide range of platforms at first and then narrow it down.

For myself, prior to transitioning I had a lot of success getting in-person clients on AdultWork and getting online clients for my porn on MyFreeCams (I did camming) and Reddit and Twitter. I rarely used any other platforms. Since transitioning, this has changed a lot. In terms of escorting, I find that SleepyBoy has been a good site for me to find clients. I still use AdultWork, but being listed under "male" means I get far less clients than I did before transitioning and I get very few inquiries from there. I also use Tryst, but I don't get much interest through the site itself and instead I find that it's most useful to use it by attaching it to other social media (like having a pinned tweet with the Tryst link that mentions meets).

On sites like Twitter, follow other transmasculine people who make online pornographic content and look at how and where they advertise. You can still use Reddit to advertise, by having links to your porn on your main profile and then posting nudes or lewds in various subreddits. You cannot mention on the post itself that you're selling porn! But, if a picture does well, people will click on your profile and some of them will subscribe. I recommend finding different porn subreddits that focus on certain traits. There's r/boypussy which has a lot of cis men on it, for example, but does allow trans men too, and it specifically for gay men posting asshole photos. There's also r/FTMPorn, r/EnbyLewds, r/bois. Take a look for yourself at which places you fit into. You can also post in non-porn subreddits where people post selfies with SFW images in the hopes that people will click on your profile.

Depending on the level of visibility you're willing to tolerate, and the amount of hateful targeting, you can use outrage about trans issues to your advantage. Make sure you have a few tweets with links to your content or escorting ads, even if you have zero followers, and a pinned tweet with all of your links. THEN, start posting in reply to things! If there's outrage about some sort of trans issue, reply to the tweet. Interact not only with other people in porn, but also in general discourse. Make sure you mark your profile as 18+ and that you have that in your bio, as well as making it so that your images are marked as sensitive content, so that no-one will accidentally see porn without deciding to if they click on your profile.

When speaking to medical professionals:

Do not tell your gender therapist about your involvement in sex work. Leave it out, if you're seeing a gender therapist to get a diagnosis of gender dysphoria, when you are asked questions about your attractions or sex life. Some would be fine about it and supportive, but it isn't worth the risk that your involvement in sex work will be seen as evidence that you are not truly dysphoric or that you're too unstable to be approved for things like HRT or surgery.

When getting STI tests, especially if you sell sex in person, I recommend going to specifically trans clinics. There is such an overlap between trans people and sex workers that most clinics set up to cater to trans people which also do STI tests will be supportive about your involvement. You can request that the information you give them is not shared with your GP, so even if they were to be judgmental it won't impact your healthcare in the long-term. Check with places near you. I would personally recommend both TransPlus and 56 Dean Street, if you live in the UK and you can get to London. Otherwise, do your research for trans clinics near you that offer STI screenings.

If you're selling sex directly, or are using the front hole a lot in general for videos, keep an eye on whether you're experiencing vaginal atrophy or dryness. In a case where you are, talk to a doctor about it. Topical estrogen that's localized can work to fix it without changing your overall hormone levels.

Also important if you're selling sex in-person – get on PrEP if it makes sense for you, and keep in mind that if you're having front hole sex then you need to take it every day and it only starts working after 7 days of taking it. The rules are different depending on the type of sex you're having!

Working while recovering from top surgery:

Plan in advance as much as possible!

If you sell sex, expect not to be able to see clients for a minimum of 2 months after surgery. Any regular clients should be informed of this in advance if possible. You can use the upcoming surgery, and the fact you will be unavailable for a while, to push people to book you whilst you're still available. Particularly, clients who like the fact you have breasts are likely to book you before that happens. Depending on your branding and popularity, you may be able to raise your rates in the months leading up to surgery, if you are openly trans.

Regarding online content, bulk-film prior to surgery so that you can keep posting content whilst you recover. You will be unable to film for the first couple of weeks, because you're recovering and still replenishing blood and will be very fatigued and unable to lift your arms. If you're not cleared for strenuous activity, masturbation and sex definitely count! After a few weeks, you may be able to film slow-paced content. I would recommend that if you do film during this time, because you couldn't create enough before surgery and need to post to keep interest, that you make videos like "first time getting off post-surgery" which go slowly and aren't strenuous. Viewers will understand, you get to make some very niche content, and the intrigue will keep them subscribed or keep them buying videos as they wait for you to fully recover.

How to handle chasers:

You need to make a decision early on about how you're going to handle clients who are chasers. If you're selling porn, many of your viewers will be chasers and there will be nothing you can do about it. You can block people who post chaser-y and fetishizing comments on your posts on social media, but that's the most you can do to keep them away, and in doing so you will lose business. If you sell sex in person, you have a little more wiggle-room, but chasers will still make up a huge chunk of your clients and cannot be entirely filtered out.

Decide your boundaries and stick to them, then reassess after some time has passed. If, for example, you have not had top surgery and don't want to take off your binder for porn videos or when having sex with clients, you can set that as a boundary. You will not make as much money, but you can set a firm rule about it and then later assess whether it's something you need/want to let go so that you can earn more. If misgendering of any kind is a hard line for you, you can put that on your profile and tell clients outright if it happens, blocking people from your subscription porn services if they do it or leaving bookings in person if it occurs and you feel safe to do so. Have a plan in place for each type of disrespect or for each physical boundary you have.

Some chasers may be willing to contribute money for things like surgery or hormone therapy. Others may be willing to buy you certain toys or equipment, like a strap-on or an stp (stand-to-pee device). You can take advantage of this by making mention of things you want, and even saying how you would use these things in a sexual context. If you want a packer, use rolled-up socks in your boxers and mention that you want a better one. Create a wishlist of transition-related things you want and then let clients know about it.

Interacting with other sex workers:

A lot of sex worker spaces will not be made with you in mind. They will be created for cis women first and foremost, and trans people of all kinds will be an afterthought. Be aware of this and don't assume that because sex worker organizers have generally progressive views that they will all be supportive of trans people. If you do not pass, you are likely to be lumped in with women, and if you do pass then people are likely to distrust you (even when you tell them you're trans).

Find community with other trans sex workers first and foremost. Do not only association yourself with other transmasculine people, but also with trans women and transfeminine people, and non-binary people who don't have an affinity for any direction. Other trans people are the most likely to know where you can find the resources and support you need, and also to understand you and your gender. Pay attention to the trans women around you, and what places are hostile to them… then have solidarity, even if those places claim to support you. We are stronger together. A transmisogynistic group which claims to support you when you do not pass or as a transmasculine person who is not (yet) transitioning will turn on you too, as soon as you pass or assert that you're not a woman a little too strongly for their liking.

All of that being said, there are many groups which are predominantly cis women that are genuinely accepting of trans people and it is vital that you work with them and talk to the people in them. Sex workers are a vast community. Gender will impact our experiences, but we have so many in common. Seek out groups that are predominantly cis gay men in sex work, too – there are journalists and researchers who write about gay male experiences in sex work and there are trans men among them.

Above all, keep in mind that you're not alone. It's hard to find trans men or transmasculine non-binary people talking about our experiences selling sex, even though there are many of us, because we're thrown into other groups. We aren't hypervisible the way that trans women are in sex work, which means we're not targeted for violence in the same ways but also means that it's hard to find people discussing it. Either we're lumped in with gay men in sex work when we pass and are dismissed, or are lumped in with cis women in sex work when we do not.

So many of us aren't speaking. You're under no obligation to be one of those who does, but you should also keep in mind that your experience is valuable to hear about.

Thank You!

To everyone who supported the creation of this anthology, allowing the contributors to be paid, I would like to offer my thanks.

I'd also like to acknowledge the friends I've made in my local sex worker community, who have accepted me as a trans person and as a sex worker and whom I feel entirely at home with. I could not have made this book without you.

To Sidney, Jorge and John, thank you for letting me rant about the creation of this anthology with all of you. Obviously you couldn't escape my ramblings, because we live together, but the sentiment of appreciation is still there!

To one particular friend on Discord, who supported me through making this and helped me draft e-mails to contributors and listed to my struggles, your encouragement has meant a lot to me.

Through supporting the Kickstarter to raise funds for the publication, this book was able to be created and published as a result of community support. Here are the names of some of the people who made **Working Guys: A Transmasculine Anthology** possible, and those they have decided to dedicate this book to:

Ollie Campbell
Rachel McDonald
Stevie Carroll
Alix
Saint Dionysus
Danie W

Halone & Avi
Razz
Roopot
AJ Bravo
Jeremy Wiggins
Foster McKinnell
Jesper D
Joey Evergreen
Jessie Nguyen
David Kozat
Emilina
Sinnaka Elena Fitzgerald
Sophia Woerner
Mnemosyne Iah Delaney
Isaiah Whisner
Giuseppe
Gender Community Lending Library
Silva Neves
Sabrina Aermeda Page
Andreas Meichelböck
Ioannis
A. Marie
Tania Glyde
Rosie
Lou Stutz
Carter Crystal
Peter Flockhart
Cas Nova
Booker-Garet Feniks
Nathan E
Scarlett Wilkie
Han
Elizabeth S
Petrichor

Kailin B
Ellenor Carlson
Zakariya Ziani
Mochi
Elvys Ehlum
Randall Hudson
Sunshine Castleford
Alex Sanderson-Shortt
Isabella "Ted" McDonald
Katy
Francis Woods
Skylar Bastedo
Joamette Gil
Michael B

Stay up to date with future publications from Jack Parker by signing up to their newsletter at jackviolet.com.

www.ingramcontent.com/pod-product-compliance
Lightning Source LLC
Chambersburg PA
CBHW051258020426
42333CB00026B/3252